It Happened on Purpose

Value Yourself Without Being Full of Yourself

PAUL R. ROY

Copyright © 2016 Paul R. Roy

All rights reserved. No part of this publication may be reproduced, stored in a retrieval system, or transmitted in any form or by any means, electronic, mechanical, photocopying, recording or otherwise, without the prior written permission of the author.

The author has tried to recreate events, locales and conversations from their memories of them. In order to maintain their anonymity in some instances, the author has changed the names of individuals and places, the author, may have also changed some identifying characteristics and details such as physical properties, occupations and places of residence.

Layout and Design by Oak Island Publications
oakislandpublications@gmail.com
Cover design by Marianne Curtis

Published by Paul R. Roy
Published in Canada

Paperback
ISBN: 1537058754
ISBN-13:978-1537058757

CONTENTS

	Acknowledgments	i
1	Winning the Birth Lottery	1
2	Am I the Problem?	7
3	Seeking Recognition	13
4	In the Trenches	19
5	Living the Dream	27
6	Chasing the Dream	33
7	The Dream Takes Flight	39
8	Bucket and Cape	45
9	Humble Pie	53
10	And They're Off	61
11	Getting Traction	69
12	Things Start to Slip	77
13	The First AHa	83
14	The Darkest Time	91
15	It Gets Better	97
16	Leaving Land	105

17	Dealing with Mom	111
18	It Happened on Purpose	117
19	Pivotal Books	123
20	I Can Make a Difference	129
21	Brotherly Love	135
22	I Trust You	143
23	Seven Guests	149
24	Measuring Up	157
25	Peeking over the Horizon	165
	Paul's Principles	167
	About the Author	173

*The wind will blow you in the direction it wants,
unless you know how to adjust your sails.*

ACKNOWLEDGEMENTS

I have read so many impactful books in my life that they have helped mould me to who I am today. The old adage that a setback is a lesson rings true leading us to who we are and will become. I love public speaking and the book was at first a vehicle in which to gather speaking engagements. It has become so much more. I made the decision that the book needed to stand on its own, as a success unto itself. I enjoyed the process so much so that I have two more books planned.

I struggled with the notion of how someone who failed English twice while in high school could write a book. I learned a few things in my life and going to the pros when you know you don't have that skill set is always a good choice. That being said I wanted this to be one hundred percent my words and short of grammar, structure and spelling edits they are.

My book writing coach Les Kletke is in himself an inspiration as well as an author. His technique in pulling the story and message out of me so I could piece each chapter together saved me from writer's block. I could not wait to dive into the next chapter. It was after writing chapter six that Les said "congratulations! You're now a writer." I will never forget those words Les. Thank You.

I met my editor Joscelyn Duffy, when she was doing the editing on a short story I wrote for another book project *The Gift Of The Hit*, in which I was a contributing author. I was impressed with her writing style and I knew it was Joscelyn who I would want to do my edits. She herself is an international ghostwriter and creative and she knew what it would take to give my story that extra polish. Thank you for your support and encouragement. You inspire me.

Marianne Curtis is also a best-selling author and chief creator at Oak Island Publications who pulled together an amazing theme for the front cover. I learned from Marianne that it's also the presentation of the words that gives additional impact. Marianne was and is a huge help guiding me through the steps of self-publishing. Marianne. You're the Queen of Clarity.

CHAPTER ONE

WINNING THE BIRTH LOTTERY

Key Concept:
Longevity = Love + Purpose

Good roots create a huge advantage in life. They set the stage to start on your way up the ladder before a word comes out of your mouth. Born the third of four children, I came into this world smack in the middle of the baby boomer generation. I had the good fortune to grow up in a happy and active family. I was the son of a successful doctor, who took after his father. My mother was a stay at home mom. She was the daughter of a successful businessman. She managed her own financial affairs with the efficiency of a CFO. Investing in the stock market was her passion. Mother kept things orderly in her ledger, just as she did for our family affairs. We were certainly a family of achievers. There was no middle of the road in our house. Adventure and life lessons awaited us every day. There were two schools in our house: the one we attended five days a week, and the school of life. My parents wouldn't have had it any other way.

The good fortune of being born into my family brought with it a lifestyle in the upper middle class. We lived in a great neighborhood in Halifax, Nova Scotia, surrounded by successful families. Across the street was the Senior Vice President of one of Canada's biggest breweries. Around the corner was one of the city of Halifax's most successful developers. Our next door neighbor was a successful lawyer who sat on many corporate boards and was an advisor to two of Canada's Prime Ministers – Lester Pearson and Pierre Trudeau.

At a young age, I was a very good sailor, winning the provincial (state) championships at various levels. I was a competitive skier and raced on the provincial team. I dreamed of being on the National Ski Team, but my best years racing came late, in my late teens. Sailing became my passion and has taken me to many parts of the world, both competitively, as well as recreational. I have raced to Bermuda twice, competed in seventeen Marblehead races between Boston and Halifax, cruised in the Mediterranean and the Caribbean Sea on several occasions and sailed down the coast of West Africa in a Transatlantic Yacht Race. I am fortunate to live on the ocean today and keep my boat in front of my house.

Growing up, we belonged to all the 'right' prestigious clubs – The Yacht Club in the city, the Best Family Summer Club, the Saturday afternoon Family YMCA and the Curling Club. Not only did we belong to these sports clubs, we also held season tickets to the symphony and local theatre productions. My parent's friends were wide and diverse. It was all part of their master plan to raise well-rounded kids to set forth into the world.

We had all the things we ever needed. Mom and Dad kept us fulfilled with new skis, bicycles, musical instruments, hockey equipment and the latest version of sailing crafts. To enjoy these things, we needed to perform in school and our music. We adhered to the time set aside to study and practice our instruments. I played the trumpet, attending private lessons each week and playing in the city youth band. Needless to say, we didn't have the time to get in trouble.

One might think with all the toys my parents afforded us that I was given money. Not so. If I wanted money, I had to earn it. I had a healthy appetite for cash, so I did. I mowed lawns in the summer months and shoveled driveways and walkways in the winter months. I worked as a junior councellor at the YMCA after school and taught sailing in the summer months once I was sixteen.

The same rules applied to play time in the yard or at the summer club: I was to practice my trumpet thirty minutes a day, six days a week. During this time, I can attest that it wasn't easy listening to the other children in the neighborhood out playing hockey in the street or shooting hoops. There were days I wanted to throw the trumpet away and run away. I sometimes hated being taken to the symphony by my parents. I was often the only youngster there and didn't enjoy the music. My practice paid off as I won the trumpet section in the city music festival one year and played on closing night. The irony of all these music lessons was the day I no longer had to practice, I began to enjoy symphony music.

I had a woodworking business I ran out of the basement while I was in high school. It was just another step in my journey to becoming an entrepreneur. A neighbor and member of a rug-hooking and needlepoint group was telling me it was difficult to find frames required to stretch the material. This was back in the day before huge craft stores began popping up to service the craft types. I saw this as an opportunity to turn a profit. I liked doing physical things, and making rug hooking frames seemed simple enough. My dad enjoyed woodworking as a hobby so the necessary equipment was at my disposal.

The first twenty years of my life gave me a great understanding of self-discipline and a solid work ethic. I have struggled with delayed gratification most of my life, however, my determination and preparedness to do what was needed to succeed and achieve my goals always rose to the forefront. This attitude became the cause of some pain, knowing that if I over-extended myself, I would need to do what was required to right the ship. I watched my father go to the hospital on many a Christmas day to check in on his patients. He truly cared and was a doctor because he loved being a doctor. The money was a nice side benefit. It was his commitment to his job that I remember most. Thanks to my upbringing, I have achieved many of my life goals. I can directly connect this success to my parent's insistence that only I am accountable for my success.

Money was not provided for education in our home. It was believed that if you wanted to go bad enough, you would find a way. Mom and Dad would be supportive through encouragement and they would find other ways to help financially. My father told me when I was in high school, "I'm not giving you one red cent for university." You should be in business. You have the people skills and the drive to be a success. He was right. I couldn't wait to graduate from high school and get to work, gaining the skills I needed to own and run my own business.

The social network of my parents provided me the privilege to meet many influential people in both the private and public sectors. I loved hanging out and meeting successful people. I was like a sponge. I learned to emulate them, and they became the fuel on my road to achieving success. Many of my high school friends were the sons and daughters of extraordinary people. Real Estate moguls, construction heads, distribution company owners and the like. The sailing community was also a source of meeting achievers. As a teenager, I crewed on their boats and yachts. I wanted their lifestyle, and I knew that if I was going to have it, I would have to earn it. I wasn't afraid of the challenge. I looked forward to it.

At the age of 26, my father and father-in-law loaned me the money to buy my first business. They became preferred shareholders with financial terms much like a bank. The most important thing I learned from them was that it's the mentors and the successful people I looked up who were more valuable than the money that fueled me. It was proof in point that if you want it bad enough, you will find a way to make it work.

I believe that hard work can be a great equalizer. It's important to work smart. It's equally important to work hard. Sixty-five-hour work weeks became the norm in my life. One little thing I liked to do was go down to my store on Sunday mornings before church. I'd wash the windows and the front of the building. I enjoyed a clean look but I also wanted the community to see I took pride in my business. I was rewarded by being elected the Chair of the Downtown Business Association. A position I held for two years, before I was thirty years of age. I volunteered whenever I could. I chaired the Stewarts at my church. I was a Kinsmen. I believed beyond a shadow of doubt that if you give you will receive.

Yes, I came from two families of privilege. It would have been easy to pretend I was entitled to a soft and good life. Not so. I lived in a town where my Grandfather had been Mayor. He owned the newspaper among other businesses. There was, however a generation between Grandfather and myself. I needed to prove to the community I was worthy of their support. I was anything but lazy. The town in which we lived was a blue collar town. There were no gimmies. You had to earn your support. You can't buy respect. It's earned.

Success is only impossible if you believe that to be so. It's tough to sustain an easy lifestyle over the long term. Though, it will catch up to you. There is no template for success, other than to keep trying until you succeed. Failures create determination if you look at them as building blocks. Perseverance is probably the biggest asset a business person can have. We must have a purpose. It's the foundation to a successful and happy life. We have all heard it takes 10,000 hours to excel at our career or job. That doesn't happen on easy street.

Before my grandfather built his successful businesses he went broke in the 1920's, when the shipbuilding business and the age of sail was overtaken by steel and steamers. The multi-generation family business went bankrupt. Grandfather started his new business selling hardware from a horse and buggy. From that he repaid his debts and ended up owning seven successful businesses throughout his business career. That took guts and self-discipline. It is also said the best revenge is success. I know this to be true as I have lived this myself. I watched my doctor father start a business after he had to retire from medical practice at the age of sixty-five. His retirement plan included working. I plan to do the same, as I believe having love and a purpose in life leads to a long life. It's not work when you look at it that way.

Longevity = Love + Purpose

The medical and statistician experts will tell you that if you are in a loving relationship and you are productively working toward your purpose, you should then live a long life. If your purpose for the day is to mow the lawn, as important as it is…you might want to rethink it!

CHAPTER TWO

AM I THE PROBLEM?

Key Concept:
Our interactions are as unique as we are as individuals.

It was no secret that I didn't like school. I was in and out of trouble in the classroom. I made regular trips to the principal's office for acting up in class. Because of this, my parents created rules and they lived by them. They saw this as the only way to deal with my unruly energy problem. They kept me in every possible extracurricular activity to keep me out of trouble, but it wasn't working. They struggled with the fact that I had an older brother who was immensely bright and skipped two grades through school. My older sister and younger brother also seemed to ace school. The only possible solution was to turn down the screws and keep me on a tight leash.

Mom and Dad were trying their best, but by the time I was a twelve, my view of purpose in the world was not even in the same hemisphere as my parents. School was a punishment in itself, let alone having strict rules placed on my daily activities. I thought I was thinking clearly, but I couldn't manage to understand my concentration issues. I failed to understand why restricting my sports time and other things I liked to do would help me in school.

Even at this young age, I began to live my life as what I thought was normal. I found ways to work around the rules to stimulate my need to burn my excess energy. My bicycle always saw extra duty. It was my freedom to cruise the city and explore. Mom and Dad had restricted my TV time. That made no difference, as TV bored me. I would watch the first five minutes of a television show to get the situation, then head out and shoot hockey pucks against the garage for twenty minutes. I would later come back in the house to watch the last five minutes of the show to see the conclusion. The twenty minutes in the middle of the show seemed like meaningless fluff. Details bored me to death. Why did the adult world insist on inserting all the stuff in the middle when the solution was is right under their noses? It all seemed pointless to me at twelve years old.

I learned what I liked and didn't like at a very young age. Pushing back and acting out created a bigger hole for me to climb out of, and I didn't give a shit. A pattern was beginning to develop. From my perspective, it was to keep it simple and make sure I have a chance to burn off this excess energy. The thing that began to rattle around in the back of my young mind was how could I remember the complete events of a day that happened a month ago and not remember what I read in a book ten minutes ago. It was baffling.

I excelled at whatever sport I played. The hand-eye coordination, coupled with my desire to be the best, was very fulfilling for me. In my younger years, hockey was my sport of choice. Every winter, I would make a skating rink in the back yard and tend to it like it like I had just purchased my first home. I scraped the ice every night and I would flood the surface with water for a clean sheet to play on in the morning. I had set up flood lights so I could be out at 6:00a.m. skating and practicing. It was my palace, and my opportunity to be the best. Keep in mind this is in the early 60's. Parents rarely drove their kids to the arena like the kids of today. I played 6:00a.m. games at the Civic Arena at the far end of the city. I walked the forty minutes to the arena carrying my gear, as the busses didn't run at that time of day on a Saturday. My dad always gave me the twenty-five cents for the bus ride home.

In grade five, hockey was taken away from me. My father had told me if I wasn't in the top four in my class with my marks I could no longer play organized hockey. It was the beginning of a period where I felt my father was the meanest prick on earth. I was devastated.

Of course, the music lessons had to continue. My afternoons at the YMCA continued. At that time, sailing became a big part of my life. It was dad's first love and only natural that I follow in his footsteps. Sailing also got me out of the house five days a week for lessons. Sailing was competitive, fueling my passion to be the best. It stimulated all my abilities, was physically demanding and gave me the uncanny ability of reading the wind patterns. Sailboat racing was also about knowing where to go to take the best advantage of wind directions and velocities. Sailing is a four month a year sport in Eastern Canada and the souring effects of being without hockey in the winter months was devastating.

Still weighing heavy on my young mind was why was I so good at sports and terrible in school. On second thought, I was good at anything that stimulated me. I had some good years in school when I had engaging teachers. Their teaching styles had an impact on my results. I was beginning to understand my shortcomings. In those times, kids could not pick their teachers, so schooling became a roller coaster ride for both my parents and myself.

Mom and Dad did not know what to do about my 'hyperactive' problem, other than to send me off for a barrage of mental tests. This was back before the days when ADD was recognized as a condition. I spent hours with the Psychiatrist. This was something you didn't broadcast around the schoolyard. All very hush. If that news got out, my life would be in ruins. The sessions with the therapists drove a wedge between my father and me. I hated them. My skilled paediatric physician father had two problems to deal with: he struggled with the fact he had a son with what appeared to be a learning problem, and he couldn't figure out what the problem was. The result: I ended up being medicated to tone down all the excess energy I possessed.

I was a square peg trying to fit into a round hole. Organized structure was my mental enemy. My concentration levels created a big problem with both my studies and home life. School totally bored me. Every now and then, I would get a fantastic teacher and I would be at the top of the class. This education seesaw went on for all my whole school life. What was discovered from the tests is that I had a very high IQ. 128 to be exact. My IQ scores are in the top four percent of the population. I wasn't dumb by any shape of the imagination. Get my interest and I would remember every word; bore me, and I was at the bottom of the pile.

I had ended up in summer school a few times over the years, thanks to a classic example of a teacher who was determined to undermine my success. I worked with my tutor who helped me with my homework and scored all my essays with good marks. The unruly English teacher I had saw otherwise, often giving me a failing grade. To make matters worse, I broke my wrist playing baseball in the school yard just a week before final exams in grade eleven. Said English teacher determined I would do my English exam orally. Not only that, he had a substitute teacher sit with the class while they wrote the exam so he could do the exam orally with me. He gave me a forty-eight and I failed. Former Prime Minister Pierre Trudeau used to say, "Oh Fuddle Duddle." My expression of disappointment bore words not worthy of being repeated. The result being I needed to go to summer school so I could move to the next level. On the first day of summer school, the teacher said to me "What are you doing here"? You shouldn't be here. I ended up helping some foreign students learn English so they could attend university that fall. My only obligation to the class was to read and do my book reports. I passed my summer course with flying colors.

I managed to play a lot of hooky my first year at high school. I lived at the pool hall on Quinpool Road. A choice I later came to regret. The extra year afforded me along with a few other wayward students to go to the local tavern each Friday's at noon for lunch in my grade twelve year. A beer and a wing steak for $2.99. Yes. We were of legal drinking age. I hated the high school experience so much I didn't even attend the graduation ceremonies. My life behind bars had finally come to an uneventful close.

It was clear that if I had a teacher that could stimulate me, I would pass with flying colors. I truly believe after my schooling experience, we as a society need to rethink education. One size does not fit all, and finding the right teacher for an ADD like me was like playing the lottery. It seems that such high intelligence as mine could easily be cast aside as a misfit. Those with ADD have many amazing talents that could at times put the other students in a state of bringing up the rear.

Think of the problems high energy, high intelligent types like myself would have working in an office environment that is very process orientated. Typically, one must follow the job description or risk losing their job. We want to be part of the team and be appreciated for our abilities. We need to be comfortable in having a conversation with our managers about what stimulates us. We want to produce and have an impact on results. Often, the results can be the same, however completed via a different path. When our managers know our strengths and weaknesses we actually make their jobs easier.

For intelligent and energy-rich people like myself, it is important to understand who we are. We should have a good grasp on what stimulates us and have a clear understanding of how we interact with the people around us who don't see the same view as we do. We can reduce the possible negative impact we have on fellow workers. I had my grade six views on life for a long time, and I certainly felt like the square peg trying to fit into the round hole. With some good guidance and understanding of our strengths anything is possible.

Our interactions are as unique as we are as individuals.

Of the 7.4 billion humans on this planet, no two people are the same. The same can be said for our relationships. No two are a carbon copy. One of the bonuses of an ADD is people skills. We find ways to connect and create meaningful relationships. The default choice of buyers is to purchase services and products from people they like and trust...or maybe that's just my ADD.....

CHAPTER THREE

SEEKING RECOGNITION

Key Concept:
Sometimes, you just have to sit on the deck of the boat with a wobbly pop.

The removal of organized hockey from my life was a difficult process for me to wrap my head around. To a Canadian kid in the 1960's and 70's, hockey was gospel. I think my father knew what he had done by removing hockey; however, he didn't back down. I sensed he knew I was hurting, but he remained uncertain if his strict policy on school results was going to work.

I grew up being taught to be the best in all aspects in your life. Dad was competitive. That trait had trickled down to me in everything I did… with the exception of school. My older brother, Peter, excelled in whatever he set his heart to. It tended to be more cerebral for him. My sister Barbara performed well in school and became a competitive sailor. My younger brother John did well in school as well as excelled in sports. Things seemed to come naturally to all my siblings. I was the black sheep, becoming known as the troublemaker at school.

Dad knew I needed an outlet for all my excess energy. I had a cousin Bob in Toronto who was a world class skier on the Ontario Ski Team, later becoming a member of the Canadian National Ski

Team. He and his parents had been sending along his used equipment for me. My neighbors had a decent size hill in their backyard. Both neighbors across the street had taken an interest in my skiing, seeing me out there practicing. They used to take me to bigger local ski hill in Wentworth on the weekends. I worked on my skills and dreamed of following in cousin Bob's footsteps to be a skier of some talent. One day, while skiing at another local hill, the coach of the provincial team noticed me and asked me to train with them. He said I could perhaps become a member of the provincial team. I managed to place third one year in the Eastern Championships and was Club Champion at my local club.

Skiing had become my new winter outlet for all that abundance of energy I possessed and it filled my competitive spirit. During the summer months, I excelled at sailing. It played into my ADD in a positive way. It allowed me to keenly know my surroundings, to take them in, and to understand where the competitors were on the race course and who was on the favourable tack. I could feel the speed of the boat under my rear end, and I knew when the boat was lively or moving along like lumpy gravy. Sailing to me was multi-tasking on steroids. It challenged my intelligence and it fueled me to become a provincial champion on three occasions at the age brackets during my middle teen years. Sailing was my chance to really be a *somebody*.

My teen years were spent on smaller sailing type skiffs. My father always had a large sailboat that I used to sail on as well. Dad's love of the sea was infectious. He had the ability to break away from the competitive racing as we often headed out cruising the Atlantic coast spending the nights in secluded coves.

Big boat racing was where the action was. My sailing abilities brought me opportunities to be the driver in the big boat game. Work opportunities came from gentlemen who were not the best helmsmen or drivers. I was picked up to sail one such boat when I turned twenty years old. My abilities afforded me the chance to grow my talent and to sail even bigger and faster boats. Sailing was a very social affair, which played into my talents as a people-person.

Sailing brought me the recognition that I wanted, and it puffed dad's feathers as well. He too was provincial champion in the Snipe class in his teen years. Younger brother John was equally as talented as me and we came to the agreement that he was a better small boat sailor and me the better big boat sailor. That competitiveness between us drove us both.

The interesting part of sailboat racing is that it attracts successful business people to a gentlemen's sport that is extremely competitive. Many of whom like me desired the recognition winning brings. Their egos were fueled by owning the fastest boat and having their name go on the trophy even if they didn't drive the boat. For me, it was about recognition from my peers, knowing that I was a damn good helmsman. I believe no matter what we do in life, there is no greater honor than being recognized by our peers.

I agree the competitiveness filled my feel good tank. Everything boiled down to me hating to lose more than I liked winning. Everyone likes to win. Hating to lose trumps liking to win every time. I learned to control my temper with age, but it always still stung when we didn't win. There was always a lesson in losing. It gave me the chance to analyse what went wrong. I tacked away when I should have stayed the course. Experience came from knowing where the puffs of fresh wind came from. We sailors jokingly call them 'Private Idaho's.' "Look at that bugger go," they would say. "He is pointing higher toward the mark and going like a bat out of hell." Paying very close attention to those things became part of my skill set for winning sail boat races.

In my twenties, I found that school was always running in the back of my mind. Would I have been a great doctor instead of being an insurance salesman? It was during that time in my life I knew I would have made a great doctor. A great doctor with an excellent bedside manner. A doctor whose patients revered him just like my father patients adored him. It stung that I didn't follow my father's career path. I had laid my bed and I was learning to live with the consequences of being a poor student, and not a doctor. Business had become a great second choice for me – a choice I later learned became the fuel for me to become a success… to be a somebody.

I was beginning to learn that all the losses in my life, whether in the classroom or the racecourse, were lessons. However, I wasn't out looking for losses to be able to learn more. My rush-in attitude along with rush to closure tendencies had left in its wake enough grief for both my parents and myself. I came to realize that I performed better as a result of my past losses. For anyone that has read Malcolm Gladwell's book *The Outliers,* it is evident that to be an expert you need to have trained, practised or competed for a minimum of 10,000 hours to be among the top in your field. My losses became fewer as a result. Winning became a much higher percentage of all the starts as a result of what I learned from my losses. Practice does make for perfect, or close to!

Watching sailboat racing for the non-sailor is about as exciting as watching grass grow. The speed measurement used for all things that move on the ocean is termed as a knot. One knot of speed is 1.15 miles per hour. Boiled right down sailboat racing is a game of 1/10 of a mile an hour. A good sailboat moves along at six to eight nautical miles per hour in good wind conditions. For example, the bi-annual race from Boston, Massachusetts to Halifax, Nova Scotia is 360 nautical miles in length. If we were to say the average speed was seven knots, it would take 51.4 hours to complete the race. If your average speed was 7.1 knots it would take 50.7 hours. Roughly forty-five minutes over the course of the race. That's huge. You don't win sailboat races by tying down the sheets and having a wobbly pop. You win by making those micro adjustments to constantly win races.

With age, I didn't enjoy the competitive racing as much. I did it for fifty years. I still head out on the race course, but the need to prove myself is long gone. One beauty of sailing is that you can keep doing it long past the competitiveness had gone over the horizon. Spending a day on the water is one of the best chill outs you can enjoy. The wind and the warmth of the sun on your face is very therapeutic. The squalls and rain can dampen the day, however we can't control the weather. The camaraderie can be enjoyed just as much while delivering the yacht to the next race venue as the race event itself. Sailors have a bond to the sea and all people that love the sea. A good sailor is never afraid of the sea and its fury. We learn to respect its power and give thanks to its countless joys

Sailing taught me to be in the moment. Everything happens there. It can be like a chess match, but imagine changing the layout of the chess board in the middle of the game. In racing, the conditions are changing all the time. You have no choice but to be in the moment. The same applies to business. You have to know where you are at any particular time. From there you have the ideal situation to make sound decisions about moving forward. It may not always be the right decision and like sailboat racing you can always tack away when the winds or the tide become unfavourable. It's not about 'Plan B,' but rather an adjustment to 'Plan A.' The new and improved 'Plan A.'

Offshore racing is a beast all onto itself. In many cases a gruelling test of endurance and mental tact. How does one remain alert for twenty-four hours a day? Pre-race planning becomes imperative. The navigator studies the weather and tide conditions. He, along with the skipper choose a likely route to take the passage. Most offshore racing boats will race with a complement of eight to fourteen crew depending on the size of the yacht. The crew gets split port and starboard watches. That means you're on deck for three hours and below deck resting or sleeping the other three hours. You're expected to give one-hundred percent when you're on deck. It's intense only if you want to win. If I'm going sailboat racing I go to win. I had been fortunate enough to be on teams over the years that felt the same way. We won many a race in the wee hours of the morning, with pouring rain pounding against our faces, as the rest of the competitors were struggling to stay awake or looking for cover.

Communications on the team is key. Each crew member has a speciality much the same as in a business environment. Operations doesn't do well in sales and the sales team are usually barred from messing with operations. The same applies afloat. It's a team effort. The spinnaker trimmers and the driver were in constant verbal communication often talking to each other about the trim of the sails. If the driver wanted to surf a wave to gain speed, it required the trimmers to adjust the sails in unison with the driver adjusting the course. The navigator always mindful of the direction the yacht is headed keeps us going in the right direction. Boat speed means nothing if you're going fast in the wrong direction. Communications and talent win yacht races.

We often hear in business that we need to have the right people on the bus. It's true, we also need the right people on the boat. The desire to win is a sought after trait for yacht skippers. It's equally important to have the right people in the right seats paired with that desire. The term 'team' is used less nowadays in business jargon, as there has been a shift to being best we individually can be. To that I say *bunk*. The value of a team is greater than the sum of the parts.

Sometimes, you just have to sit on the deck of the boat with a wobbly pop

It is said that families that eat together, stay together. The same can be said for sailors who compete together. Win or lose in this case the relationship is usually cemented with an adult beverage. The sport and the competitiveness create both business and personal relationships that sail on through the decades.

CHAPTER FOUR

IN THE TRENCHES

Key Concept:
Progress = Perception + Mental toughness

Poor results in my school marks meant I was going straight to work. I wasn't that upset. I hated studying. Studying with more school would delay my success in business. I knew I had the desire to succeed, so I wasn't afraid. I had always managed to make money as a youngster and I was convinced I could do the same as an adult. Going to university would have meant I would have to wait for the things I wanted. I wanted my own apartment, a car, and the cash to support my busy social life. Going to work was a good thing.

I knew that I would need business skills to be a success. I felt the business world would become my education and a platform for me on my way to owning my own business down the road. The early years would be my apprentice years. I moved through several jobs to obtain those skills. The upside of not going to university was very clear to me. I would be making money while I was learning. That made a lot of sense to me, and it would support a lifestyle that I wanted. If I was going to be my own boss, what would it matter if I had a Bachelor of Arts degree? The old adage that if we keep telling ourselves something enough times we would believe it to be true even if it wasn't.

I was convinced this direction of learning the skills in the trenches of the business world would become the foundation for my life. I wanted to be a business success like my grandfather. My grandfather didn't have an education so why did I need one. Success was embedded in my mind. I did realize at that time that laser vision was a common trait of someone with ADD. Many of us can focus intensely on a goal and go after it. It wasn't until later in life that I would appreciate how lucky I am to have all this intelligence and energy.

I visualized what it would be like to be a success. That image remains indelibly printed in my mind even today. The fancy cars and waterfront homes were things I knew I would acquire. I didn't have the luxury of moving up through the ranks of a family business. My father was a doctor. I would have to do it the old fashioned way and earn it!

I started looking for work the day after school was out. I was nineteen years old and I hit the streets looking for a role in the financial sector. Within a week, I was employed at a collection agency tracking down people who didn't pay their bills. I didn't realize until a few years later what I learned here would be crucial to my success in my business career. After a year, I moved into the money-lending business with a finance company. Sadly, the borrowers paid a higher interest rate because of the increased risk of being repaid and it was a hard business to be in. I later entered the insurance world with a commission-based job and was attracted to this business and the concept of being paid directly for your results. It was the first step to being self-employed. My business tool box was filling up.

In the first week of working at the finance company, I had to do my first repossession. I went with one of the more senior people in the office. We first went to rent a truck so we could carry all the goods that were financed and well behind in their payments. The home was located in a public housing complex and we were to collect some furniture and appliances. Can you imagine how I felt asking them to take the plates off the kitchen table so we could collect the table and chairs? We also collected the washer and dryer but that didn't hit me as hard as the kitchen table. That moment of time in my life has remained with me some forty years later as a lesson about paying your bills.

I looked at this experience and wondered how they allowed themselves to get into that position. These people I thought weren't fortunate enough to have grown up in the way I grew up. I felt pity for these people not having a role model to guide them in their early years. I saw them as trapped without the ability to break free from the cycle. It became clear to me that our school system focuses on the three 'Rs' without planting the seed to break-free. School is important; but life skills are ever more important.

Being a bill collector is much like being a detective. Many of these people were late on their bills and also have other unpaid debts. These debtors didn't have phones and if they did their number was unlisted. We had to find people the old fashioned way. Tracking these people down could be tough. I would visit their last known address. I'd knock on the neighbors' doors asking if they knew where they had moved. Checking with the employer on record when they borrowed the money and working it backwards from there. It rarely was easy. I learned to be persistent in tracking down the leads always mindful it would get me a step closer to collecting the money and closing the file.

The satisfaction in tracking them down brought on a great feeling of accomplishment, not to mention keeping your job was dependent on your success. Be successful, or be fired. As you can imagine, it wasn't the job for everyone. Being a bill collector provided me with a great deal of grit. It gave me the ability to do the really hard and sticky stuff – the stuff no one else wanted to do. You don't learn these skills in university. These skills are learned by being an apprentice. I learned to be kind and thoughtful. I learned to know when they were lying and when they were telling the truth.

One of funniest repossession stories happened when a customer had fallen four payments behind on his pickup truck. I had given him a deadline to be in my office and to make payment by 2:00p.m., or I was going to repossess their truck. As you might have guessed, he didn't show. Two of us from the office had hopped in the manager's car and headed out to get the truck. The debtor came out of the house when we arrived and threw the keys at us. "She's all your guys." He had taken the wheels off and the truck was on blocks. The only way to get the truck back was to call a wrecking truck. That we did.

In my business life, I learned that a slow-payer became a reason to have a conversation with a customer. It became an opportunity to measure their satisfaction level with our business. I have learned to pick up the phone and have a conversation. Emails can be deadly, and I avoid them when the topic has the potential to be sticky. The internet has afforded people without the guts to say their name to post harmful comments. It's wrong, and I won't read a news article where you may comment and not take ownership. I see these people as gutless wimps. Thumping away at your position of the facts will get you nowhere. Your customer's perception is their reality. Yes, the customer is always right, even when they are wrong.

The old adage you can catch more flies with honey than with vinegar rings true in the business world. I learned in my bill collecting years that kindness allowed the conversation to be less threatening and easier to move the issue to a consensus. Heavy handedness will lead to your customer feeling threatened and they will certainly push back. No one wants to deal with a bully. Get rid of the I'll show you attitude and your results will soar. I also found a bit of light humor was effective in dropping down the wall the debtor built as a protection mechanism. I always found that kindness and understanding moved us to the top of their list to be paid. The bonus being it made me feel better because it was the right thing to do.

Many of these debtors had other outstanding bills to pay. Empathy became a trump card for me. I often floated to the top to be paid. Caring for someone under the difficult circumstances they usually created will win the day. I remembered because I was different than all the other bill collectors who made demands. Remember the guy with the pickup truck on blocks? I got heavy-handed and made a demand. A little kindness might have got me the truck with the tires and rims still attached. Wisdom is earned through experience.

I found one of the best methods for collecting past due balances was asking the customer to remark on the bill collector's work. I would ask the customer, "John, I noticed you haven't paid your bill yet. Is it something we did wrong? Are you unhappy with our service?" This technique totally disarms the customer as we have not cornered him or her putting them in an uncomfortable position. The answer I usually got was "Paul, I'm really sorry. I have been really busy and overlooked paying your bill. I will put a cheque in the mail today." Nine times out of ten, they did. I kept the customer. I let them off the hook. Every now and then they would remark on the service or lack of and I was there to hear it. It afforded me the opportunity to make our business better. This was a bill collecting activity and a customer satisfaction survey all wrapped up into one.

Getting my business degree on the front lines of business was the best thing for me, as someone with ADD. Activity-based learning provided me with the people skills you didn't learn in the classroom. In all the businesses I have owned or been a partner in, I was on the front line. I was the face of the business. I always advised my staff to send unhappy customers to me so we could have a conversation. Knowing your customers at a personal level builds rapport. The book *How To Win Friends and Influence People* by Dale Carnegie is a must-read for all business people. It was while reading this book I became aware I was already practising many of Mr. Carnegie's recommendations. Skills I learned on the front lines of business.

The irony is, I now love to read. Most of my reading is about how to improve myself. Books that will give me more leverage in business situations. Life I believe is about constantly learning. It's like golf. Some days you leave the eighteenth hole mumbling that damn game. We debate giving up, but we don't. It keeps bringing us back because we want to be better tomorrow than we were today. Isn't life grand? We can't go through life being a spectator. We must go out and live it.

Empathy is one of the strongest attributes we can possess. Our customers sometimes feel pain in their life or their business. I offer assistance whenever I can. I can usually put them at ease when I tell them that I have been broke twice in my life, and I lived to tell about it. "What can I do to help you?" I ask.

One situation like this actually inspired me to go and get my coaching certification. I had helped a customer go through a business transformation from a big and unprofitable company to smaller and profitable one. I was rewarded by being made a director of the company and my customer now has a fantastic business the he runs instead of the business running him. It was an absolute joy to see him take flight. If you want referrals for your business, do the unexpected. Be unique and stand out from the crowd.

In the B-to-B business world you really become a bank for your customers. In my office products business I would have $60,000 to $80,000 in accounts receivable owning to me at any one time. Issuing credit was critical to growing your business. My bill collecting years stood me well, as over the course of a year I would issue credit to my commercial customers an amount of at least a half million dollars. I wrote off less than $2,000 per year in bad debts. I credit this success to the school of front line business learning.

Mental toughness is a learned skill and keeping procrastination at bay can be a challenge. We procrastinate because we don't like to do something. You have to have a system and make the selling calls a priority. You must get comfortable with doing the tuff stuff first in the day. Yes there are days the phone weighs one-hundred pounds. You're scared to death to make the ask for their business. Once you become proficient at it you will move that daily exercise from a 'have to,' to a 'choose to' activity. Learning can be fun. Schedule a few hours a week to your personal development. It's difficult to grow your business if you remain the same old you. Over the years I have had an accountability partner. We all have had the empty feeling when we say we would do something and we don't. Being accountable is a cornerstone of success.

Progress = Perception + Mental toughness

In the selling world we learn quickly that the customer's perception is reality. Once we understand their perceptions we gain progress. It's the mental toughness of understanding their point of view where the real gains are made.

CHAPTER FIVE

LIVING THE DREAM

Key Concept:
Ask and you shall receive

Seven years had passed since I hit the streets looking for my first job in the business world. I became a graduate from the school of hard knocks and learned a bundle in the process. The credit business was a great learning experience and having to earn my own way as a commissioned salesperson in the insurance business at age twenty-three was a feat unto itself. I was also newly married and our first child arrived five days after our first anniversary. I was growing up fast.

The dream of owning my own business was always running in the back of my mind. I knew it would happen, and if I could make that happen in my grandfather's home town I would be on top of the world. I didn't think it strange that a city boy was eager to move back to a midsize town. The notion of being a big fish in a small town didn't enter my mind. All I dreamed of was being a success. Being a somebody and all of the trappings that come with success. It's a shame my grandfather wasn't alive to watch me grow. He was a self-made success, and I wanted to be the same. I thought in my mind this was the true measure of a successful entrepreneur. I knew he would be proud of me and how I prepared myself for success.

I had been putting out feelers with friends in the business world that I was looking for a business to buy. More specifically, I was looking for a business in the small town of Bridgewater. I had learned enough over the years to know that people did not put for sale signs in the windows of their business. I had to dig. The digging showed signs that my efforts would bear fruit. I was attending a yachting regatta in Chester, Nova Scotia when I bumped into a family friend on the yacht club deck following one race. He had told me that there was a stationery business for sale just a few doors down from his business on King Street. The owner was in poor health and wanted to sell. He had given me the details of who he thought I should contact. It was one of the local accounting firms I should approach. I didn't have any difficulty convincing my wife from Lunenburg that we should buy a business just twenty minutes from her home town.

Can you imagine my delight to find this was in fact a real bricks and mortar business? It turned out both the business and the real estate was available. Things began to happen at warp speed. My father and father in law had agreed to purchase some preferred shares to help fund the deal. I borrowed money from the bank and we had a deal. Two months later, I was moving my family back to Nova Scotia and opening shop.

I spent my first year in the business learning the ins and outs and getting to know our suppliers and understanding accounting. The previous owner had come in a couple of days a week to school me on the seasonal trade. At the time, the business was mostly a card and gift shop that also sold school and office supplies. The card and gifts were important as they were cash sales; however, the challenge was in purchasing the right amount of seasonal stock so there was not allot of inventory remaining at the end of the season. My wife and business partner loved the card and gift business. She managed that part. Liz came from good business family and was no stranger to hard work. I knew if I wanted to grow this business we would need to focus on the commercial office supply business. It was time to hit the road and start selling.

My determination to succeed was showing up on the sales ledger. I was pulling in new commercial accounts from business friends in Halifax and all the way down to Barrington Passage. We had a great staff, and I learned that if we empowered them to make decisions they would be happier and remain loyal. Our trust in them paid off. Very few staff left us to take on other jobs. We afforded them some flexibility on the hours they worked. They also saw Elizabeth and I working extremely hard setting an example that we were committed to success. All the while the locals treated us as 'come from aways.' I was born in Halifax and my wife in Luneburg. The fact my Grandfather used to be mayor and Elizabeth's father a successful businessman just twenty miles away meant we had to work harder to be part of the community.

My ADD kept me laser-focused on the growth of the business. That indelible picture of success in my mind began to glow brighter each month as the sales began to increase. I was now spending as much time on the road selling as I did in the office. My selling abilities had the business growing at an aggressive rate. My passion for the business just oozed out of me. That magic number of 1 million in annual sales was there for me to grab. I also knew that just selling pencils and ruled pads in a small market wasn't going to get us there. I hired a salesman to work the road so I could grow the office furniture business. Those larger ticket items would become the solution to that enviable magic number.

The business was perfect and a great way to raise a family. I was usually in the office before 7:00a.m. and my wife would be home and get the kids off to school, then come in and manage the retail part of the business. Then go home at 3:00p.m. to be there for the kids when they arrived home from school. The business was doing well and my wife wanted to open a high end gift store in Mahone Bay a small tourist town about ten miles away. It was in a new shopping complex that looked to be very trendy. No expense was spared. It would be a natural success.

Many summers we would rent a cottage at the beach for a month. Liz would stay with the kids and I would commute to the office. We worked hard to support this lifestyle, and I spent freely. The business was growing like a weed. I would leave the office early and come to play with the kids at the beach and tend to the BBQ. Living in this part of the world with an ocean playground so close to work and beautiful home three minutes from our business was magical. We made many friends who ironically were business folks like us that had moved into the town. I expect they did for the same reasons we did. They saw an opportunity. We enjoyed a very active social life and it was rare not to be out on a Saturday night eating and drinking into the wee hours of the morning.

I also became very involved in the community. I sat on the Business Improvement District Improvement Commission. I served several years on the Downtown Business Association and two years as President. I chaired the Junior Sailing Committee at the Yacht Club. I was an active Kinsmen and Head of Stewards for our church, as I learned that in a small town we need to give back. My wife was heavily involved in Guiding at the local and provincial level. We were the model couple. Professionally, I grew to be President of the Nova Scotia Office Products Association and I was also elected to the national board of the Canadian Office Products Association. I coveted that role as it allowed me to be at the table with the biggest and best players in the industry. These were successful leaders whom I could learn a great deal from. Like my days taking business 101 on the streets of Halifax as a young man I was once again in the company of masters who could take me to the next level.

We received an interest to sell the business eight years into our run. Sales were leveling off due to the recession, free trade and new tax laws. The business was strong, but highly leveraged. The couple who wanted to buy the business wanted to move back to Bridgewater from Ontario. Our accountants suggested to us it might be a good time to sell. You could come away clear and have some money left to start another venture. We thought to ourselves what would we do in small town Nova Scotia in our late 30's with no job and a small amount of cash. We would never have the lifestyle we enjoyed working for someone else. We would certainly have a reduced lifestyle with a start-up business. My wife had no interest in moving away from Lunenburg County so our option was to keep the business.

The rationale was that if I could keep selling like I have over the past 8 years we would be fine. All we had to do was create more revenue. We would tighten the belt on spending and make the business more profitable. It was still a land of opportunity, even though the landscape was changing. I could outsell the competitors from the city and the recent invasion from the price cutting mail order stationary businesses from the United States. When cash got tight, I would just go out and sell more. I was, after all, a revenue-making machine.

My goal was to be a self-made millionaire by the age of thirty-five. In my middle thirties, I was well north of $750,000 in net worth. I could see the goal in sight. It shone like a beacon. This was back in the 80's, where in today's dollar value I would be worth much more. To obtain that goal, I needed laser focus. ADD makes it easy to want to be a part of the 'rush in' crowd, asking questions later. I had always managed to learn and worked on improving myself. All my self-discipline was devoted to sales. I was always focusing on the big picture.

Sixty-hour work weeks were the norm for me. I was usually at the office before 7:00a.m. and the last out the door well after closing time. Throw in a few hours on Saturdays and Sundays and that was the life of a businessman. I always found time to be with the kids on weekends and get them to hockey tournaments and practices. Unlike my dad, I would support them in hockey while chasing the Canadian dream. During the summer I would be out on the race course, watching them grow as competitive sailors. Just like their grandfathers and father they won provincial sailing titles. The luckiest thing that happened is our boys made friends with achievers. They excelled in school and in sports. I made many friends in business that helped us grow. The reason I was successful in sales was my unrelenting drive, but most importantly, my relationships. Deep down, I knew that without those relationships I could not achieve my ultimate goal.

To this day, I am a very Blue Sky kind of guy. I didn't like the small stagnant details. I suppose, this is why I embrace change. My management style allowed their desires to be the best they could be to flourish. This allowed me to be out forging new relationships on the front lines creating new customers. The recurring monthly orders from these new customers would keep the business growing. It wasn't always easy. Like sailing, the wind direction can change and your position in the race changes as a result of that wind shift. If you focus on the all the waves between you and the horizon, you will most certainly felt every wave making you ultimately ill. That being said, the way to avoid sea sickness on the ocean is to keep staring at the horizon. That is where the goal lies.

Ask and you shall receive

Be it seeking something you want, or a finding a solution, answers rarely come out of thin air. They usually come after you have asked a question. The best sales people on this planet ask questions many times before they ask for the sale.

CHAPTER SIX

CHASING THE DREAM

Key Concept:
Oh, shiny things!

Being a success has always been a motivator for me. Like many of you, I dreamt of owning fine things and being in the company of affluent people. More than anything, I wanted to be noted as a winner in the business arena as well as sporting venues. Every person on the planet wants some form of recognition be it appreciated for our work or leadership in our volunteer efforts. I sought this more than the average bloke. It wasn't conceit. I was often advised by head hunters while looking for opportunities that I don't sell myself enough. My belief is if you have to ask for recognition you don't deserve it. My deepest desire was to earn it.

My goal of being a self-made millionaire by the time I was thirty-five had been imprinted on my mind for a very long time. I was determined to achieve it. To me, there was no greater achievement than one-million in sales annually and then one-million in net worth to follow. They were big round numbers with two commas in them. I had been told by the experts that first million is the hardest to achieve, and the following millions come easier, once you have figured out the formula. I knew it would be hard work and that didn't scare me. I had never been accused of being a slacker. I read all the latest releases of business books looking for every tip on success I could. I was completely single-minded.

I had this vision in my mind that all the money would get me the toys I wanted for me and my family. I did after all grow up in a lifestyle that needed a good amount of money to support. I vowed to be more successful than my parents and grandfather before me. Owning a nice home at the right address was at the top of the list. I had the fancy car right out of high school. We took winter vacations and spent summers at the beach. The kids got sailing lessons. There were annual ski trips to Maine at spring break and the trips to the Rockies for Liz and myself. One-million a year in sales would provide us all of these riches.

That big number was my singular goal. With that number I could obtain all I wanted. I could achieve this through hard work and smart business decisions. That big number fit right into my blue sky big picture mind of mine. I could after all employ others to look after the details. If money ran short I would just go out and sell more. I was Superman. I would put on the cape and tights and go make money.

The trappings of this number began to show up in my total lack for delayed gratification. My ability to raise sales revenues was always my back drop when I overspent. It took about ten years, but I was beginning to understand I had things backwards. I read that we need goals to achieve what we wanted in life. Write it down and it will happen. The part that I missed was that prosperity just wasn't about money. It had to do with heath and quality time with family and friends. My value system was all screwed up. I wasn't a bad person. I thought I was a great father.

In 1990, the 'arse came out of her,' as they say in Newfoundland. The world as I knew it crashed. I was broke, and I left family and the bank holding some of the losses. I was chasing my goals. I was following the advice of the experts. I worked hard and tightened my financial belt.

I became a rudderless ship, and I got turned away from setting goals for the next twelve years. My one-million-dollar target had turned me into a creature I didn't like. Goal setting became a bunch of bunk. I needed to figure out a way that I could prove to the world that I am worth my salt. This business collapse was caused from external forces. Free trade and the invasion of the American's super stores was the cause of my demise. I fought that notion off for a while, but I came to the realization that I too must take ownership for the mess I had created. Years of chasing the big goal, coupled with servicing a big lifestyle was the real dagger. I gave in and quit externalizing the blame. Gulp!

I went on the road looking for a big job that would prove to the world (and more importantly, me) that I had what it takes to run a big business. Many of you who have gone through what I went through know that mainstream businesses are afraid of entrepreneurs like us. We don't conform. The establishment thinks we work too independently. Entrepreneurs are not only risk-takers, but a higher risk employee. It wasn't until later in life I came to understand entrepreneurs embrace change and it scares the hell out of the establishment. The establishment manages the heck out of risk. In spite of the odds, I pressed on and found a big job. It was a turnaround job. They needed a person with the guts to deal with the hard stuff while growing their business. This surely was the opportunity to prove myself. Once again, I had become the victim of a changing industry. Two years into the job, I got fired.

Over the following ten years, I was fired two more times (they called it 'being downsized'). Both sent me away with fair-sized cheques that launched me back into business. I went through two more business opportunities, both of which were exercises in futility. The first business I had bought into was a mature industry that later disappeared and I bailed before it got ugly. Do you remember computer paper with the holes down the side? That was a tough lesson learned in a previous life. I also purchased a franchise that would help fifty-year-old types like myself find meaningful work. If you want to put your selling skills to a test, try to sell a bunch of thirty-year-old HR professionals the value of hiring a fifty-year-old.

It's easier to push a soggy rope up a hill. My balloon had been pricked. My self-esteem was so low I put the cape and tights away forever. I thought perhaps the internet was the new money game so I went through a period of looking for easy money on the internet and it's a hateful process. I struggled with the prospect of being a spam professional. All these get rich propositions wanted your money and then they would teach you how to do what they do. Extracting money from folks looking to get rich quick really cut against my grain.

Through a networking event I met a great couple who were Neuro Linguistic Programming (NLP) professionals. Perhaps they could get my mind back on track, I thought. I didn't ever intend NLP to be my guiding light, but it helped me get past some really shitty head trash. It taught me how to focus on my positives. Things still wavered for me, but I was slowly regaining my balance. I was in and out of another job, as well as a partner in a business. I eventually sold my shares as it was not big enough to support three partners. It was fun and to get out of the business on my terms was a big plus. My business 101 learned on the streets was sinking in.

The NLP was my first real experience of looking at what my value system was. How did that tie to my goals? How did that tie into what I though others would think of me? There was always the never ending supply of chatter from that little man standing on my shoulder saying you have not earned this Paul. Thank you Bob for helping me place the first piece of the self-worth puzzle in place. Yes, I believed in myself. The importance of anchoring that belief became very clear.

Through this process I learned that goals have to be aligned with our values. If your goals are not, then the doing what you're not comfortable with will put an end to your goal. The likely hood of reaching that goal will fail miserably. Let's call it a validation process. It is life's way of insuring you're on the right track.

I learned that goals that have measurable steps are the best. These will help you feel a sense of accomplishment on your journey.

I, to this day have my goals in an excel spreadsheet with dates I want to accomplish this by. I put the date beside them when I reach them. Writing this book was one of those goals. I started three years ago and 20,000 words in, I struggled with what my story would be. My book coach helped me break it into chapters that added structure and milestones. If I had not written it down and validated the goal, you would not be reading this book today.

If you are not obtaining your goals, there can be a multitude of reasons for that. Goals are not like the book *The Secret*. Just putting it out there and letting it happen is a bunch of hogwash. You have to mentally put out your intentions, but it is your actions that will win the day. Yes, your goals are earned. One key component to goal setting is to add emotion to the goal. For example, *I will feel over the moon happy having achieved my income target of $100,000 on December 31st 2020.* You now have the emotion attached and the date associated with it, and the validation comes in.

You have four years until 2020. What will your income be each year on the road to that date? What new steps must you make today to start the ball rolling? If you don't break it down, your chance of achieving your goal will fail. Let me add that if you came up $2,000 short you did not fail. This especially true if you started out with $40,000 income in 2016. You will reach your goal in March of 2021. Was it worth it? Of course! I can stand that kind of missing the target.

The biggest transition for me was to attach a lifestyle choice that varies from a monetary focus. For example: *I will feel amazing to now be taking two months a year off to enjoy more time with my wife and family.* Do you need to have the financial capabilities to be able to do this? Of course. What is that number? These are choices that are very manageable. I learned from my challenges in chasing money there is rarely enough money if say you will do this when you have enough money. Figure out what you want, then find a way to make it work. It's that simple.

The one sure fire way to improve your percentage in achieving your goals, is to tell someone what you're going to do. How do you think you will feel when they ask you how you are making out with that goal and you have not even started yet? Why do you think Weight Watchers has been so successful all of these years? It was the weekly weigh-ins in front of the class. There's no pressure like peer pressure.

Oh, shiny things!

Crows are often referred to as intelligent birds. They just love shiny things. I get the strangest looks from people when I tell them I'm like a crow. I wonder if the crows laugh at themselves too?

CHAPTER SEVEN

THE DREAM TAKES FLIGHT

Key Concept:
Do you want to be right or happy?

It was back in the mid 1980s that I made my first trip to Ledgehill – a corporate retreat in the beautiful Annapolis Valley in Nova Scotia. The owner, Charles Bower, had put a program together in conjunction with Henson College associated with Dalhousie University. He had assembled a group of twelve entrepreneurs who would be his students over four weekends of the coming year. During our first weekend together we spent Friday evening getting to know the group. Then the first exercise we worked on Saturday morning was to write our own obituary. There is an exercise in taking a fast measure of the life you are currently living. It floored me. I soon came to realize that this was not going to be a nuts and bolts business kind of course. The course dove deep to the core values of who we are and what makes us who we are.

The exercise forced us to take stock of what our life purpose was. Were we living the life that would best reflect what we want written about us in the newspaper a couple of days after we died? Being in my mid-thirties at the time, this was not a topic I had given much thought. What would our family and friends be saying about us? What would they say about our accomplishments and who we were as a person?

I quickly came to look at myself through a different lens. The world of an entrepreneur is focused around business issues and how we will make our ventures a success. That was all very clear to me. I was at Ledgehill to hone my business skills. This was much more than I bargained for. The program was going to be about individual focus. A learning of what motivates us. Why do we make the decisions we do? For some reason I wasn't afraid. I knew with my ADD, I was different and had my unique set of values and motivators. Perhaps my 'Aha moment' was close at hand. The elusive 'magic bullet.' The mystery of who I truly was would soon be discovered. One thing for sure is I realised that nothing would be a success until I unlocked what was inside me. It became very obvious I needed to become true to myself, my authentic self.

The 'write your own obituary' exercise was a real eye opener for me. It played against my vision and perception that money was why I was in business. My goals were all related to financial outcomes. The process created a lump in my throat that was very uncomfortable. I couldn't ignore the exercise. I was forced to consider who I was, and not just the business man in me. Some twenty-five years later, that morning has stuck with me with deep gratitude. The challenge was not to be guided by what people say or will not say about you. The challenge was to live a life filled with purpose and be recognised as having made a significant contribution to family and friends.

Charlie Bower was ahead of his time. He was into the soft stuff long before the self-help business took flight. Charlie believed we could not be good leaders if we didn't know and understand our strengths and weaknesses. The shelves of bookstores all over the world today are filled with leadership books. Not so back in the 1980s. This was cutting edge stuff. Charlie took us to a place not many had ventured to go. I realized his uniqueness and loved his perspective on life. I liked his approach to the subject of self. We need to have good business plans, but more importantly, we need to be solid individuals first. I became very close to Charlie over the next few years, going to visit whenever I was anywhere close to Ledgehill. I had begun to crave his insights. It is with some remorse I didn't go to visit him during the last years of his life while he endured ALS.

Although he wasn't one, Charlie lived like a Buddhist. His early mornings were filled with chanting music as we enjoyed the breakfast prepared by the facility cook. The morning gong was sounded when it was time to assemble. Each session in the day was ushered in by the ringing of the bells. The scene from the main gathering room was in the garden with the forest as a backdrop through a wall of picture windows. We all sat in our wingback chairs set in a circle so we could all see each other much like around a campfire. Once the group had quieted down Charlie would go around the room asking each of us how we felt. This was all very unusual for us all at first. It became part of the daily routine.

We were asked how we were feeling and to share our emotions, fears and joys. We began to trust one another knowing what was said in these sessions would never leave the room. We shared our deepest fears and desires. We laughed and cried together. A bond developed among us that could not be replicated. A group dynamic had formed and we came to appreciate that we were not alone on this road of self discovery.

We had to get in touch with ourselves before we could get into the goal setting exercises. The outcomes would be different of course now that our emotions were clearer. We had discovered what we really wanted, and that it was not all about business. I had my own set of issues going on with business struggles. I had become attached to my emotions like never before, however a successful business was still my primary objective. That is where my goals pointed. As I had stated in my goals setting chapter my purpose was not aligned with my goals and it was not until later years this became clear to me. Ledgehill was my Chapter 1 in understanding myself. I came to realise I had much introspective work to do.

All of this self-awareness exercise had helped me to become a better salesperson. I was a business owner, but my strong suit was selling. I had learned to make my passion visible to my prospects and to make an emotional attachment to the selling process. Long gone were the days of selling from your Rolodex. Back before the electronic era, we kept all our client and prospect information on a wheel that lived on our desk. We would send out birthday cards and Christmas cards in the mail wishing them well. It was all artificial. It sure wasn't me. I managed to make it personal through phone calls or written letters away from the dates that you become the center of attention.

This method of communication allowed me to connect with my customers on a personal level. I was the owner of the business who paid the visit and not a sales person. I got to know everyone on a personal level. I got to know their hobbies and all about their children. I got to understand what motivated them and made them feel good. One thing for sure, it was one heck of a lot more effective than putting a greeting card in the mail three days prior to their birthday or anniversary. I knew this instinctively and my introspective years at Ledgehill allowed the inner me to shine. Customers know when you care. They can sniff out a fake and determine if you are genuine. People want to buy from people they like and trust.

Relationship selling helps takes buyer remorse off the table. Your customers welcome you when you approach the subject of their needs with them. You get fewer excuses for saying no and more of a true explanation for the reason they may say no. They understand you will not push too hard for the sale. Buyer's remorse is a huge cost to business both past and present. I wasn't the highest performing salesman for new business when I was in the insurance business, but my business stayed on the books. I received the National Quality Award each year I was in the insurance business for business retention. This achievement cannot be achieved when there is buyer's remorse. Authenticity and trust will win the day every time. You just need to trust and embrace that concept. It will stand you well over the years.

We need to inform our customers of the options and allow them to make a decision on their timetable. Creating a false sense of urgency destroys trust. They know then the sale is about you and not them. All the sales tactics in the manuals don't teach you this. If the trial close doesn't work, then go to the assumptive close and so on. I say bunk to that. You need a selling process, but it should never interfere with the customer's respect. They naturally want to buy from you if you are genuine. Never sit by the phone waiting for it to ring. If you have made enough quality touches and your pipeline is full buyers will contact you when they are ready.

It's easy for me as a seasoned pro in the selling business to say be patient. If you have done your homework, and you made your sales calls, life will be good to you. Business is business so get past the fear of rejection. How many times have you heard selling is a numbers game? It's right. Being good at it increases your success rate. A full prospect list that has what you sell under consideration will make your phone ring because you were patient. The I want to think about it crowd will from time to time pick up the phone in spite of what the sales manuals tell you.

Today's world is all about measure it. I personally can't stand it, but today's business climate is all about serving the shareholder. Wall Street is run by numbers so sales managers are asking salespeople to be administrators of their activities. Sales people inherently hate doing paper work. I know a few successful sales organizations who hire administrators to do the detail and reporting work for the salespeople so the salespeople can do what they do best. Sell! It's not rocket science. It's just a bitch to measure, that's all. If you like it, and you work at it, you will be successful. It will become second nature to you. Goal setting works best when there are steps to achieving the goal. When you find your sweet spot you will know it and so will your customers.

If it's not right for the client, then it's not right for you either. Doing what is right wins the day every time. Do you want to be right, or do you want to be happy? The answer to that question is - look at things from the customer's perspective. They are always right, even when they are wrong. If we educate the customer so they can make an informed buying decision. We understand the emotional attachment, they will buy if there is a valid business reason. The 'I want to think about it' is not always an objection. Some customers will take longer to say yes and their decision making process needs to be respected.

When the client is happy you will know about it. You will become fulfilled knowing you have brought them to this conclusion through respect and trust. Miller Hieman's *Consultative Selling* was one of the best courses I ever took relating to sales. I wholeheartedly bought into the concept. I later became a certified as a Sales Trainer for their custom program for my then employer that has stood me well over time. What a wonderful gift to be able to navigate a conversation with a customer that has a mutual benefit to all concerned. The bonus from selling with respect and consultation is you will get many referrals because of your non-threatening approach. Trust the process and be patient is my recommendation.

One thing for sure is that from the business part of my obituary there are two words I am confident will appear: trusted and respected. I always put the customer's interests before my own, and that was a key part of my success.

Do you want to be right or happy?

Ledgehill was on the leading edge. The pointy edge of the wedge is where all the cutting gets done. These new concepts and paradigm shifts I often refer to as the bleeding edge!! Occasionally we must put away the 'I'm right' and pretend we're happy... if only for a short time!

CHAPTER EIGHT

BUCKET AND CAPE

Key Concept:
We need the lows to see the possibilities.

The North American Free Trade Agreement forever changed the retail landscape of Canada in the late 1980s. It ushered in the invasion of the U.S. Office Supply super stores. From my perspective, America is a competitive low-price battlefield. They played hard ball, turning the office products business into a grocery supermarket model: high sales volume with fast inventory turns. They turned what used to be high profit items like file folders and rules pads into commodities sold at ridiculously low margins as lost leaders. For the smaller operations like mine, the profits from those items allowed us to carry the slower turning items and be a full service business. I knew we were in for a fight on the office products end, and also as a shopping mall was being built a couple hundred yards from our business. We were in for a storm of epic proportions.

I served on the National Board of the Canadian Office Products Association and we were concerned on several fronts. Our association membership revenues were at risk once our members would be going out of business. We were running seminars and training sessions on how to weather the invasion. I felt privileged to be on the front edge of this learning process and to be learning how to compete in the new competitive environment. I was also a member of a buying and purchasing group that worked very hard to ensure we were buying at the right price to combat the skinny margins. I got rid of my fancy car and cut out all the excess benefits. We held sales to get cash for older and slower moving inventory. Operating in the same way we did for the last seven years was not an option. We also made the choice to close the second retail store in neighboring Mahone Bay that was operating marginally at best.

All of our efforts slowed the bleeding, but our margins were in free fall. Over a period of eighteen-month our gross profit went from thirty-six percent to twenty-five percent. That was to be the cash that pays the mortgage and staff. We had a third less to operate the business on. It was a double-edged sword because sales were sliding because of the new competition. It was akin to being diagnosed with a life-threatening illness. The odds were stacked against us… yet we kept trying.

Customers were making decisions based on cost, and not the impact they were causing to local business. I keep thinking of the Walmart model. They were selling to the blue collar workers based on low prices. The irony of it all was these workers were supporting the very company that was putting their production factories out of business. I'm fortunate to now be in a position not to support these lower cost import products. I don't buy from Walmart for that very reason. The global economy does not have a conscience. It's fueled by the lowest price model. I felt it first-hand, as a steady stream of cars drove by my front door on their way to the big mall across the river and to the huge business park subsidised by my tax dollars. I was heavily involved with politics and sat on the executive riding for the Conservative Party and also one of their fund raisers. I felt like a hypocrite supporting a party that was doing all in its power to put me out of business. I had enough. I quit politics, never to get involved again.

It was very difficult not to feel like a victim. Why was this happening to me? I didn't pick this fight. The pressures to perform were immense. I had young children at home, and I was determined not to let the pressure make its way in the front door. I went through a mental exercise every day when I left the office. I had an imaginary bucket and I used to unload all my frustrations and fears. Once home, I would mentally take that bucket out and set it by the garage door so not to take my business problems in the house. The kids knew it was hard, and we would often say we couldn't afford to take a trip or buy a new piece of hockey equipment.

The sixty to seventy-hour work weeks were crippling and really played havoc with my self-esteem. I was losing weight from the stress and hitting the booze pretty hard too. It was my way of dulling the pain. I also had the pressure of not being able to live up to the commitments to my shareholder family members. I was letting them down. My credibility was being held to task. To be truthful, it was with the support of family and some very close friends that I managed to keep my wits and keep from going totally off the rails. I did end up in the hospital one day with severe heart palpitations caused by the brutal stress and anxiety caused by the situation. I was thirty-eight years old and thought I was tougher than nails. I came to find out that I wasn't bullet proof after all. I did manage to avoid a heart attack, but the scars of this period of my life remained with me. It is said life is a lesson. I would much prefer to go through other character building exercises than the one I was living at the period of my life.

We tugged and pulled looking for a solution to the situation. The thought of selling surfaced on a couple of occasions. We looked hard at changing the whole business model to go back into just retail. Both those options were not acceptable to myself and my wife at that time. What would we do for a living if we sold? We still had time on our hands. I was convinced there was an answer. I spent countless hours pouring over the financials and considering all the *what if*s. It was beginning to look hopeless.

I always had a great relationship with my bank. They were the source of funds that supported our rapid growth. They were very supportive of all the work we were putting in to make this stay afloat. They do though have their limits. This was back in the days when banks took one's character into consideration when lending money. They would stretch the limits for borrowers of good character. It's a much different banking game today. The banks want your first-born and excessive security to cover the debt. I laugh now just thinking about the changes over the years. I look at banks today as organizations that loan you an umbrella on a sunny day and want it back when it's raining.

When the tough time started I always kept the bank in the loop. The branch was right next to my building so I would frequently drop by the manager's office after making a deposit just to let him know what we were doing to trim the fat and strengthen the balance sheet. My bank never played hardball with me even in the hard times. They knew I would not hide from a problem. I always had an open line of communication with them. I had created a rapport and they trusted me. Thank goodness as the difficult times of the late 1980s would have been excruciating had my banker carried a big stick. Never in my whole life was I so thankful for the honest character and upbringing provided me in my youth. Being from good stock was a blessing.

I remembered a conversation with my banker a year earlier, before things started to get tight. He said to me, "Paul you used to have great cash flow and a nice balance sheet before you opened the store in Mahone Bay. Why don't you give that some thought and call me back in a week and let me know what you plan to do." Needless to say, the decision to close the store was made. In hindsight, we should have done it sooner. Gerry was the best banker I ever had. He knew I had the answers inside me. He had such a wonderful way of making his point of view known.

I had mentioned trimming the fat from the expense side of the ledger. Downsizing my car was one of the toughest decisions I ever made. It was part of my statement of success. I had always owned big woody wagons: an Oldsmobile Custom Cruisers and a Mercury

Grand Marquis were my statement. I also had an Audi at one point in my life, and I remembered my father in law asking me after I purchased it, "Are you looking for more competition Paul?" "That car says you're in a lucrative business." The bloody bastard was right. My belt tightening car became a four-year-old midsize Chevy Citation wagon. It didn't even have air conditioning.

My close friends knew I was suffering. They knew I was in the struggle of my life. A couple of my friends offered me loans to help through the situation and I did on a couple occasions take a short term loan from them that I always repaid in a week or two. These gestures of support from my friends helped me with my struggling self-esteem. I couldn't help thinking from time to time what would my grandfather do if faced once again with a struggle of this magnitude. The successful business I had built was under attack by the American invasion and a massive consolidation of the office products industry similar to the hardware business which was facing industry consolidation at the same time. My good character could not withstand the onslaught. I put my tights and cape away, never to be worn again.

It had become obvious that throwing more cash at this thing was not going to solve the problem. We could not service the debt we already had. One painfully obvious thing I learned was that the longer you wait to do something the fewer options you have. Each day, there were challenging and gut wrenching decisions that had to be made to keep the ship afloat. The balancing act as to what suppliers were paid first during times of tight cash left us vulnerable to holes in the inventory because suppliers wanted invoices over sixty days old paid before they would ship their orders. Ensuring we stayed inside the bank lending agreement for outstanding receivables and current inventory needed to be tightly monitored. Our accounting was at that time computerized but tracking inventory was a manual operation. Running a successful office supply business was challenging enough without adding the weight of crisis cash management. I became accustomed to making these daily decisions, because waiting was not an option. I could reduce the inventory levels and create more cash and smaller payables by buying from wholesalers, but the profit margins were smaller creating a bigger problem.

I also had to be careful not to make too many emotional decisions. Knee-jerk reactions to a supplier who was playing difficult would get you nowhere. They would work with you if you worked with them. They not only wanted to sell you their products they wanted equally as much for you to pay your invoices. I had to be cognizant to think things through as each decision could negatively impact a relationship with other suppliers. I finally got to understand the pressure stock traders on the floor of the New York Stock Exchange have making million dollar decisions in split seconds. It seemed to make my job easy in comparison. This was all a first time adventure for me. The Business 101 basics I had learned on the street in my early business carrier helped me understand credit. The importance of keeping good credit, and living up to my commitments became a daily burden. Being late paying my business bills played heavy on my conscience.

Short of the bank, family and close friends the tenuous financial position of the company was pretty much held under wraps. The daily ritual of picking up the bucket at the garage door on my way to work became a way of life for that period. I developed a tough outer veneer and I rarely allowed the inner stress to be visible. I just did it. There was no other option. I pushed back the 'why me,' 'it's not fair' mentality. I worked hard and I worked smarter. I was doing all the things possible to last out the storm. Sadly, it was looking like the light at the end of the tunnel was in fact a freight train. The light was becoming blindingly closer by the day.

We need the lows to see the possibilities.

When we are at the bottom there is nowhere to look but up. The bell curve demonstrates the life cycle of your business or your life. The biggest challenge in life is regain the bounce before you hit bottom.

CHAPTER NINE

HUMBLE PIE

Key Concept:
Let honesty and integrity lead.

The writing was on the wall. We had looked at several ways to keep the business going and I had made the decision that we would not borrow any more money to prop it up. Downsizing the business to be just a retail business would mean going back to sales levels below what they were when we had purchased it almost eleven years earlier. Sure, there was value in the real estate, but I just couldn't see myself standing at the cash register of a light stationery, card and gift shop. To me, that seemed the same as owning a convenience store, where folks bought milk pop and chips.

The logical outcome was to focus on how to wind things up and try to come clean with the bank. I had been keeping the bank in the loop all the way through our struggles and they were very supportive and did not seem to be in a state of panic. They were not eager to push the button and force us into bankruptcy. That would mean that they would have to absorb the costs of appointing an insolvency auditor and that would likely mean they would have to wait longer for their money and most likely receive a smaller amount of money after costs. They liked me enough and trusted me enough to wind up the company and handle the closure. I had personal guarantees along with my father so they felt they were in a safe place.

Over the past four or five months, I had had several friends with talent and expertise come to our assistance. They included a lawyer and former senior banker. I felt blessed to have such friends willing to donate their time to help us through this gruelling ordeal. We examined all the numbers and options. We looked at who might be the best suitor to perhaps buy the business and save the company name and more importantly our pride. This was after all, the town where my Grandfather had been mayor and bringing such embarrassment to both families would be unbearable.

We opened negotiations with a company ninety miles from our business. We were in the same buying group and had attended conventions and buying group meetings over the previous several years. They were bigger than us and also in the photocopier business. They were under assault like us on the office supply side; however, the copier business and the contract office furniture revenue would surely help them weather the storm. We shared everything we could to get them to the comfort zone. Every last bit of detail down to customer lists and our inventory was provided to them. The suitor also saw us as a way to expand their copier sales and contract furniture sales, adding roughly a fifty percent increase in market size. They would operate under our brand name and we would avoid insolvency. The embarrassment of going broke would be averted. My friend David the ex-banker had helped us hatch a deal. He was my Houdini. The company had even offered me a job to work with them. It looked like we had managed to stop the light at the end of the tunnel from advancing toward us.

Our suitors suddenly went mute. They stopped communicating in the middle of negotiating a price. A couple of days later they said they were unable to make the deal work. I was in a state of shock. The goddamn thing was going to collapse. It looked like things were going to unravel. The top was now off the blender and things would get messy. Needless to say, I was very nervous about making the trip up the street to tell my bank the deal with our suitor was off. I was prepared to run the white flag up the pole and surrender. The lump in my throat was so big I could hardly swallow. I informed the bank that we were no longer viable and that we were turning the assets of the company over to them the next day. To this day, the stress was so unbearable I can't remember all the small details of what took place over those days. To make matters worse, the company who I shared all our information with in hopes they would buy us at a bargain price had gone to the bank and claimed they would buy the name and the inventory and reopen the business as a subsidiary of their parent company. Short of the doors being closed for one day, it would look like they purchased a going concern. This man had been a friend. I trusted him. The bastard jammed me.

Wrapping up a business is much like being an executor of a will but for one difference. You have to deal with the debt and not assets. We were left owing the bank a fair sum of money following the closure and our competitors injection to buy the assets and receivables. In the weeks that followed, I worked to ensure we pulled in all the accounts receivable so we could pay down the bank. Once again we worked at hatching a deal to settle with our suppliers who were in behind the bank with a settlement to avoid insolvency. Everyone came to the dance, except Revenue Canada. They demanded all the money. We could not make that happen so the settlement offers fell apart. The dream was over. I had managed to lose close to one million dollars in assets in three short years. I had managed to win the battles over the years but eventually lost the war. I had gone from hero to zero. There wasn't a rock big enough for me to crawl under.

My father-in-law was insistent we see that the local suppliers like the radio station, the newspaper, the oil company would all be paid. "You will still be living in this town Paul. They will respect you for this." He too would be affected by this business failure as it was his daughter who was a partner in the business. He did not want his name tarnished either. He was one tough businessman and he understood the complexities of being successful in small town Nova Scotia. He was a mentor of mine. I used to call him the Marshmallow with Sharks Teeth. You couldn't bullshit him and if you did he would eat you alive. If you were genuinely hurting, you couldn't meet a gentler kinder man.

He asked me how much I needed to clean up the company and personal bills around town. He wrote me a check and said, "We can work out the details later." One has to be careful in doing this as it could be construed as favoring suppliers and could cause trouble in the settlement of the total outstanding debt with the bank and our suppliers. I went to all of them and handed them cash and asked for a hand written receipt paid in full by me and not the company. They had, after all, made good money from me for years as I supported their businesses. I was able to look them in the eye and say thank you. I told them I was sorry. Some had tears in their eyes. My eyes were damp too.

Our children needed to be able to go to school and not be ridiculed on the school yard. In the big picture, it wasn't a lot of money but it was probably the biggest and the wisest thing we could do if we were to remain living in the town. At the very least they would say we were honorable.

My mother and father's families were successful business people for generations before me. My father-in-law was hugely successful in his own right. He was a self-made millionaire like my grandfather. I remember well when the investment firm Smith Barney used to run a television ad acted by John Houseman. The closing line of the ad was, "They made money the old fashioned way. They earned it." I saw this as our family names being tarnished by my inability to also be a success and uphold with honor those who went before me. How would I be able to own another business. Who would hire someone like me who had failed? However, I knew that many successful people had failed many times before they were a financial success. That was so far down the road it didn't even seem relevant.

I was advised by many friends that this was inevitable. It wasn't my fault. I saw this as being ordinary. I wasn't ordinary. I was better than the rest, or so I thought. Until you have lived through such anguish as a business failure, you really don't know pain. It's very different than losing a loved one. They take a piece of your heart when they leave you. When you lose a business in public fashion it takes away your pride, your self-worth and your self-esteem. I can assure you there is no greater pain. It's a different type of grieving. Yes, this was largely the result of industry consolidation. Forces beyond my control ended my dream. Just ask the tens of thousands of companies put out of business by Walmart. It wasn't their fault. They got squashed. Sometimes life just isn't fair.

I had to clean up this mess I left behind as best I could, because I needed to move forward and get on with my life. I needed to be a good father to my children, someone who they look up to. It became painfully obvious this wasn't just about me. This was an exercise in humility that I would come to learn later brought me more strength and resolve. It wasn't just a character builder, but it helped my children too. Just try to get your head wrapped around that notion when you're, re penniless and not knowing where your next dollar will come from.

To my disbelief, I was being approached by companies to come and work for them. There was another offer from the owner of the company who jammed me on the sale of the business. My honor and credibility would not let me work for such a man who would do that to me. Successful business types and friends from sailing community had approached me and I agreed to one offer to become an investment broker with his firm. I thought it would be a great way to once again reach my goal of becoming a millionaire albeit ten years behind my target date. I was just about finished the securities course, when I came to the realization that I would be years in the trenches earning my stripes before I would become a success. The lifestyle I built would have been shoved back more than I would be willing to accept. It meant moving away from the beautiful home we had and back to the city. I didn't complete the course, deciding to go look for a big job that would pay me what I was worth and prove to the world I had what it took to run a successful business.

I came to learn through this excruciatingly painful process that I could never go wrong doing the honorable thing. This lesson would come back into my life on several occasions. I was learning to understand who I was to the core. The upbringing from my parents and lessons I learned along the way, that being honorable is the only way to a good night's sleep. Yes, you will have some restless nights coming to a resolve with your problems and issues, but doing what is right wins the day. We shouldn't comprise our core values. Find other ways to compromise in your life. Never with your core values and your honor though!

The business world is cruel as there will always be those who want to wrestle away what you have so they can have more. I have learned never to try to win at the expense of others. Earn your business based on what your value proposition is. During my toughest hours after losing the business, I had friends appear to help me. They donated their time and expertise to try to make this work. In the week following my business failure I had over $20,000 appear from friends and family with the simple message. "You will need this money to carry on and find your way." There was no need to pay them back, they said. "This amount of money will not change our lives. You and Elizabeth need it." I was so humbled by these gestures of kindness and caring. I had to fight back the feelings that this was charity. In this moment of darkness, I came to realize this was happening to me because of my good character.

The world view is that we have to be responsible for our actions. Take away the injury lawyers who will try to convince you it's someone else's fault. I had all the excuses for being a victim of circumstance. I got mowed down by the big corporations. The struggle was in being honest with myself and accepting some of the responsibility. I could not let go of those feelings. I could not embrace that thought of being the right guy in a situation gone very wrong. I could not deny it happened and I had to move on. I needed a clear head. I needed to regain the *can do* attitude that got me to this stage of my life. I had to stop licking my wounds. Through some serious soul-searching and time, I would convince myself and my family that I was worth it.

Love of family trumps everything. Integrity stands on it's own and is also a big component of love. We can't be truly trusted unless we have integrity. My success in business today is founded on this belief. This belief is supported by a conversation with my banker on the last day before signing off. After the guarantees were met, I stilled owed them over $35,000 that would not be repaid.

He said to me, "Don't go away Paul. We still want you to be a customer for your personal banking needs. This was a business deal with a very bad ending. You have handled this with open and complete honesty." I remained with this bank for years to follow. I have not allowed honesty and integrity to cloud my judgement to this very day. Thank you, Mom and Dad.

Let honesty and integrity lead

Doing what's right wins the day every time. It's in the long game where our values and principles are deeply rooted. Trust is transferable by way of a referral, however, it ultimately has to be earned.

CHAPTER TEN

AND THEY'RE OFF

Key Concept:
Find out who is really the boss.

The cash from our friends and family was starting to dry up. I had passed on a career opportunity with a securities firm because of my impatient belief that it would take too long to build a sustainable business. Six months had passed and I was starting to get anxious from the constant reminders from my wife about the status of our bank account. Elizabeth's father created a job for her at his business and that was helping to pay the bills. He also offered me a job to work in his marine shop, but I declined, seeing it as a step back. My pride got in the way.

As a business owner in Canada with more than a sixty-six percent stake in a company, you are not eligible for employment insurance benefits should your business fail. It therefore takes risk to a whole new level. I had no source of income. The property and the house never looked better, as I couldn't sit idle. Panic was starting to set in. The sting of the business loss six months earlier was eating me alive. I really needed to get to work. More importantly, I needed to find a job that would prove I wasn't a failure. I wanted to manage a successful business and vindicate myself. The prospect of finding a meaningful and challenging job was making me look to other parts of

Atlantic Canada. We loved our home and our children were happy in their schools. Like their father, they excelled in hockey and sailing. More importantly, my wife was very attached to her family and resistant to a move. I was caught in a vice.

In March, the seventh month following the loss I was approached by a headhunter to consider a job for a client she was representing in the town of Truro, Nova Scotia. The pay was good and they were in need of a General Manager that could turn the business around and grow sales. This was a real opportunity to prove I had what it takes. I pushed back the thoughts that I was raised in a family of privilege. What was I even doing considering running a race track and agricultural facility? This was a seven day a week job. The race track ran a twelve dash card every Thursday night and Sunday afternoon. I pushed past those thoughts of long days and weeks of work. The drive to prove myself was unrelenting. I accepted the challenge.

I knew Truro from my skiing days and it was only two hours from Elizabeth's hometown. We had made many friends from Truro, while on our skiing vacations over the past years. We would have instant friendships that would dull the trauma of moving to a new town. Truro was a stately town with beautiful Elm Trees that lined the streets. Heck, we were coming from Bridgewater a lumber and agricultural town. Surely there would not be much difference. I moved on ahead of the family as they waited out the school year and a summer of sailing. A new start awaited.

I really dug into the role as GM and managed to get the facility being profitable after some cost cutting measures and renegotiations of some supplier contracts. I enjoyed my daily walks in the back stretch visiting the barns and talking with the trainers and grooms. They were so passionate about their sport that one could not help but embrace life at the track. Things began to change once I learned how to read a race card. I struggled with knowing that every harness race driver was not giving their best on race day. Harness racing is a handicapped system that moves winning horses up the ranks to the next class up. These horses often could not win that class and earn no money for the next few weeks until they dropped down a class. It was common practice to see the lead horse coming down the track with the driver hauling back on the reins trying not to win. Those who know the sport know this. It's the poor unsuspecting gamblers who lost their money.

Once again, change is in the air. The cash starved Province of Nova Scotia decided to open a Casino. The gutless short sighted bastards were going to force Harness Racing out of business. We would lose all the heavy gamblers to the large wagering pool at the casino. The back stretch at this track employed over a hundred people paid indirectly from the winning purse. The supply companies like the food industry, cleaning supply companies and vets that serviced the industry we're all at risk. I had close to eighty staff on my payroll. It was a business that employed hundreds of people with a huge spin off implications and it was all at risk. The political thirst for cash put the very existence of an industry in grave danger. Shit! Here I was again a victim of change.

Needless to say, we were losing money once again. The losses were mounting up fast and we had come to the end of our credit line. The banker for the facility had called me in for a meeting to discuss the situation. I was advised the bank was not going to issue any more credit. I needed to report back in two weeks with a plan. I made what I felt were needed recommendations to the board of directors to save the facility. I was fired one week later. They advised me they were going to play political roulette with the government. They will have to give us the cash. Holy shit!

Needless to say this was front page news across newspapers in Nova Scotia. Jesus, what else could I possibly do to humiliate my family once again? I had some friends who knew the true story and reported the facts to the newspapers. I had been vindicated, but it was a consolation prize and second page news. I had been wronged and needed to avenge myself. I decided to sue the organization for wrongful dismissal. I won the case, but the damage had been done.

One of the benefits of the job was I created some great friends on the agriculture side of the business. They were after all business people like me. They understood hard work, hardship and commitment. Farmers have my greatest respect and my admiration. They are a breed all unto themselves. No pun intended!

I had suffered another crushing defeat. Working for a volunteer board is one of the most challenging jobs a person can endure. Decisions are often made from the board members hearts and not from a point of reason. That is why they are involved after all. The irony was that one of the board members accepted my job to be GM at a much lower pay rate as he was now retired. In hindsight, I saw this as the boards motive for letting me go, but they failed at making me the scapegoat for their own problems.

I managed to prove that I could make good business decisions as I did turn the facility back into a profitable position before the government kicked out the center tent pole. I earned the admiration of many of my staff and the horsemen in the back stretch. Those still faithful to my predecessor became tolerant of me knowing my intentions were admirable. I walked the grandstand each Thursday and Sunday at the track and listened to the abundance of free advice from our patrons. I always smiled with appreciation, understanding that they loved this sport. My being approachable was important to them. I listened, yet stared down my detractors as they chipped away at my edges. I knew I had the mental toughness that successful business men must endure.

Deep down, I wondered how many more of these changes in industry dynamics I could withstand. I had been blindsided twice in four years, no fault of my own other than picking the wrong area in which to participate. It happened during a planning session with my lawyer regarding the legal case with the race track. A long time friend and lawyer saw me sitting in his office. He came in and said to me, "Paul, I'm sorry to hear what has taken place with you. The next time you see a lump of shit on the ground in front of you… walk around it."

To throw more salt in the wound, my wife lost her job the same week as me. She had been working for a decorating firm and they dropped her just like that. To this day, I don't know if was related to my being fired. Small towns seemed to have their way of being cruel upon our arrival. Elizabeth had held it from me for about a week so I could deal with my issues. I cried with pain. What had I done to my family? How could I have been so wrong this time. Was it having ADD and being impatient with the board that caused this? I knew the wheels of government turn slow, but no good person deserved this much punishment.

In revisiting my accomplishments at the facility, I returned it to profit before the government pulled the rug out from under us. My leadership helped breathe some life back into the business by opening off track wagering parlours across the province to increase revenues. I added race cards from other tracks to widen the audience and increase the size of the wagering pool. The initiative brought forward by the racing commission helped remove the long periods of time between races as now patrons would have a dash happening every ten minutes instead of every twenty. These off-site facilities did bring back some of the lost gamblers and today some of these facilities still draw a crowd. I spoke at every opportunity on the radio or as a guest speaker at service clubs, creating awareness of the value of the facility. I knew my marketing skills had what it took. While I was in Truro, my long standing involvement with Rotary began. It was my way of getting connected to the community.

Volunteer boards are a necessity to many non-profit and not for profit organizations. These board members are in many instances the life blood of an organization giving of their time and in many cases their money to support their beliefs. These people are to be commended. That being said, many a successful business person will tell you that management by committee is a slippery slope. Decisions are often fraught with compromise and based on the reactions to short term issues that impact long-term good. Successful boards know the difference between governance and management. When boards don't let their General Managers or Executive Directors manage, they will struggle. Good managers will leave volunteer boards who try to manage instead of focusing on their role of governance, vision and purpose. I have so much admiration for the successful managers of these organizations because I have lived it. It's not a picnic. In fact, it's one of the most difficult jobs there is.

Facts are, things will change beyond our control. Any factory worker whose plant closes due to a change in the value of our dollar will shake their head in disbelief that what they do is no longer of any value. Losing your job to cheap overseas labour in countries that are big polluters just doesn't seem fair. I bet my job on doing what was right for the facility and for the taxpayers of my province. I paid for it by getting canned. I still hold my head high knowing I did not compromise my values for the short sightedness of the board. Add to that the shortcomings of government officials who have never run so much as a hot dog stand make multimillion dollar decisions which impact thousands of people.

It takes a special person to work in the environment of volunteer boards. These jobs can take a life of their own and often end up not being what they were hired to do. Because these organizations tend to burn through cash their hired managers become fundraisers to support the aims of the boards they work for. It can be a vicious circle. I can tell you I would never take a job like that again as I need to be involved in a controlled environment where decisions are made based on what's best for the customer in a profitable way. Profit is not a dirty word.

I was once again in the position to be looking for work. I won a lawsuit against the track, which left me the money to start another business. Where would I do that? I had become risk adverse and with good reason. Word got out that I was a good manager and an excellent marketer. I was trustworthy and stood my ground when pushed for the wrong reasons.

The phone rang from a head hunter saying they had an opportunity for me with an international marketing board. There was no guarantee, however he said I just needed to show up and meet with the board. They will hire you. It meant working for another volunteer board and I vowed I would never do that again, though it seemed like a perfect job for me. I would be marketing on the international stage jetting around the world. That job would have my family living in an area they have no attachment and in another province, which was an eight-hour drive from my wife's home town. Family won the day, and I said no to that dream job. Life, I was learning, isn't always fair. I was about to turn forty and my life was in a shambles.

Find out who is really the boss.

I'm the captain of this ship and I have my wife's permission to say so.

CHAPTER ELEVEN

GETTING TRACTION

Key Concept:
Have a unique value proposition.

After the job loss at the racetrack, it took me a couple of months to heal. I was able to collect employment insurance, but the slim pickings didn't compare to what my salary was. I was damaged goods in the job market. I began to do the hunt for a business to purchase while my lawsuit for wrongful dismissal was going on, however the months were slipping by. Anyone that has been through such an ordeal well understands the former employer will drag their feet as it all part of the plan to wear you down. I wasn't buying into that notion. I stuck it out and won the case. It was sweet revenge, but I was not allowed to make the finding public. The background noise from the case had stopped and it was settled after discovery, before we got to the courthouse. I had some breathing room.

The funds from the settlement were not enough to make an outright purchase of a business, but enough to go searching for an investor and perhaps some cash from family. To find a business large enough to have the cash flow to support our family would not be an easy task. It was by word of mouth that we had found the office products store in Bridgewater.

I had heard through the grapevine that a computer forms business was for sale in town so we started to pursue that opportunity. I managed with the help of a friendship network, to find an investor and my mother in-law helped with a small loan so we were all clear to go with the cash I had put aside from my settlement. Banks usually don't lend money for these types of business transactions because there is no bricks and mortar and large stacks of inventory for them to secure the loan. To make the deal work, the vendor agreed to take back a loan that would be payable over four years. The math worked. It all seemed doable.

The business was the retail arm of a tractor feed business forms company. It had a nice cash flow and a solid customer base. Those of us old enough to remember big corporations like Moore will know what I am talking about. The dawn of the computer age in the mid 1980s had taken hand written, manually produced work orders and cheque writing forms to computer generated business forms. This all happens with multi part paper forms produced on NCR paper, so there would be multiple copies for the various departments and of course the customer copy. It all happened on dot matrix printers.

Through the due diligence work prior to purchasing the business, we knew it was a narrow window that this technology would last. We anticipated five to six years and this would provide us the time to reinvent and embrace the next technology that comes along. The business had a recurring revenue component to it as customers would just reorder when they got low. All the negatives and proofs were kept on file and it was as simple as insuring the next set of sequential numbers appeared on each document so our customers had an audit trail of their activities.

The customer list was really what we purchased as it included an impressive group of solid companies like big oil delivery companies and prescription labels for drug stores. Revenues were in the $400,000 range and we saw had an opportunity for growth with my selling abilities. It seemed a great business to get involved with. I pictured stock rooms full of tractor feed forms. The paper with the holes down the side of it that you would tear away once printed.

I created a great relationship with the bank who were going to fund our new current receivables. All was in a good state of affairs. Things were running along smoothly for about a year when the invention of laser printers took hold. This really became a competitive threat, as it allowed traditional printers, who we called flat printers to enter the business forms arena. We set out looking for opportunities to get involved in the flat print business but it was expensive. The costs associated with acquiring printing equipment is prohibitive; add in needing the ability to finance or lease over time, as you're faced with a big challenge. We did not have the cash reserves and I was running the business out of my house. We would also be faced with going retail and finding a store front. Multi-part forms were expensive to produce and to buy. A good laser printer could produce three copies on traditional paper very rapidly and at about half the cost.

Here we were again, going down the road of industry consolidation and rapid change just like the last fifteen years of my life. Life was hard. I should have studied harder and became a doctor like my father. Some twenty years later, I see why the Change Management Consultant Business is so big. Industry shifts that used to happen over half centuries or decades now seem to happen at a much faster pace. Our average order size for printing was close to $400. This new technology would certainly take a bite out of our gross revenue. Not only did we have new competitors with the flat printers, we were faced with declining revenues because our average order size would be cut almost in half. I was embracing change, but the obstacles always seemed so insurmountable. Would this ever stop?

Truro was an agricultural town that had a great business base to service that industry. The town had numerous factories that employed hundreds of staff. Two of Nova Scotia's best known business families, the Stanfields of underwear fame and Wilsons of oil business fame were part of the town's business elite. There was also a huge carpet manufacturing facility that shipped carpet all over North America. All three of these companies were good customers. They remained very faithful to us with their printing requirements. They understood the fabric of supporting a hometown business something that didn't happen in Bridgewater. I am forever grateful for their support.

These supporters were not enough to keep us profitable and the inevitable started to happen. The man who we purchased the business from was also feeling the squeeze as he still owned the printing side of the business. He was really now a wholesale printer who printed for some of my competitors. He started to raise our prices, which put pressure on our profit margins. This forced me to start to look for suppliers out of Quebec and Ontario who were more competitive from a pricing perspective. This just added to stress for both parties and he started to suggest to his other customer to go and see so-and-so, in retaliation for the business I took away from him. Here I was paying him several thousand dollars a month for the vendor take back and he starts to squeeze me. It was getting ugly.

The whole relationship with the seller of the business became very strained. My business partner and I felt that the vendor was in breach of our non-competition clause and we had engaged the services of our lawyer to study the situation. These were desperate times and we were under extreme financial pressure. He was feeling the pinch too, so we were now playing hard ball. He hid behind the value, he is a wholesaler and needed to be fair to all his customers.

Here I was considering taking legal action. This is something totally against my grain to do. Real men do business on a handshake don't they? What is it with this town that I need the services of a lawyer to make things right just three years apart. Legal action costs money and what would we solve with this. I asked my lawyer straight up what was the chance of winning. He told me 50/50, with a cost of close to $30,000 to sue. After some soul-searching, we decided not to. It would be too risky. We were now exploring options to diversify the business, however, they all came with costs we were unable to afford. I was in the vice once again and backed into a corner faced with a decision to sell.

The dynamics of the business were changing quickly and we had no time to spare if we were going to get out with our ass intact. I was not prepared to go down the road of bankruptcy once again. I spent a month trying to find a friendly buyer of the business, but they were also feeling the pinch of consolidation. They had the luxury of being established and had lower overheads. We were left with the option of going back to the vendor and saying, "It's yours."

I was fortunate to have a great banker who trusted me and allowed us to manage out the wrapping up of the business. "You will get paid fully. We have $40,000 in receivables that I will make every effort to collect." They fully agreed this was the best way to go.

This all happened so fast I really didn't have time to hang my head and mope. I needed to save my good word. To save the honor of my family was extremely important to me. We were broke once again and out of work. In hindsight, there were red flags right from the get go. That knot in my stomach that said I'm not sure about this deal. But I was Superman, remember. I allowed myself to get that tight suit out once again. I would be able to triumph and push back the doubts with my ability to sell coupled with my great interpersonal skills. Why my wife and family stood by me all those years of hardship amazed me. I think they understood my work ethic and deep love for them.

I struggled with the notion that my whole future lay before me. One thing for certain, the world moves quickly and we need to be accepting of change. I have become an advocate and always advise other business owners to spend time working on their business and not in their business. If you are a cog in the wheel trying to save expenses you will be running with blinders on. It's so easy to get in the cost cutting mode to make the math work. Yes, running a lean business is important to being profitable, however you pay your bills from revenue, not savings. If you're spending time as the cog in the wheel you are only worth what you're paying your staff to do that function. You will be so consumed with everyday activities just doing stuff you can't see the big picture. I feel this is one of the reasons I am so successful understanding market trends today. If you get blinded enough times like I have it becomes a new instinct. Thank goodness I had learned that we are not in business to survive, but to flourish.

Having great products at great prices is not enough to be successful in today's business environment. It becomes extremely important as a small business owner to understand you can't be good at everything. If you are going to be good at anything understanding your market is the most important thing. Big or small, it doesn't matter. You are always under attack from changing markets and the person who comes up with the next best thing. There are tons of good administrators who can keep track of your numbers and your inventory. That is not where you should have your focus. These staff members should be giving you the data you need to make sound business decisions. Quit trying to be all things to your business. You're the visionary, so go be a visionary.

Business owners need to be on the leading edge of the market and technology shifts. I actually prefer to be the second guy in the game as you have a chance to determine if it's a place where you want to go. Let them make the mistakes. You are close enough to the frontrunner that many will think you're leading the market. I call this the bleeding edge. This is where all the risk hangs out. It's also where the rewards are too. My advice is never to go 'all in.' Save that for playing cards with your friends.

If you're looking for a business or a product to get involved with my advice is always to stay away from the crowd. Be careful of running with the herd. Where there is a crowd there are trends and a short market life. It's also a place fraught with competition, which means skinny profit margins. We should just put our pride of being big and flashy in a dark room and lock the door. Be content to be involved or move your business plan to a smaller and consistent market and product. That's where there are less competitors and an opportunity for profit. We pay our bills from gross profit, not gross sales.

If you're really innovative, consider creating your own blue ocean. Can you find a way to turn a mature market on its ear and in fact create a space you totally own? If this is something that peaks your interest then I suggest you read *Blue Ocean Strategy* by W. Chan Kim and Renee Maubourgne. The tag line is 'How to create an uncontested market space and make your competition irrelevant.' It sounded like a business person's dream! I know what my competition was doing, but I don't tease them or try to compete with them by offering lower prices or flashy advertisements. I searched for ways to be unique with a great value proposition. Customers seeking a product or service to solve their specific needs are not buyers of trends. They are prepared to pay a fair price.

Have a unique value proposition.

If your unique value is like finding Waldo in a picture of 1,000 people you might want to wear orange neon. Or better still, paint a new picture!

CHAPTER TWELVE

THINGS START TO SLIP

Key Concept:
Know when it's time to reinvent yourself.

The five years we spent in Truro were some of the roughest years of my life. I can't say I ever called it home. The boys weren't that happy there and their schooling was starting to suffer.

We had made a few good friends who we are still close with today. The high tide came up behind the Stanfield's plant in town, but it was anything from being ocean front. Much like our dilemma in Bridgewater, we did not see Truro as the land of opportunity. It was forever on our minds.

We had a nice home in a great area. The lots were big and just ten minutes to town. On a hot summer's night, you could hear the sing of the saw blades from the saw mill a mile down the road, though we missed the ocean. We both knew there was more to life than a piece of real estate. We decided to sell the house and get out of Truro. We needed to put the adventure behind us. We asked our realtor and neighbor to price the house so it would sell. It sold in two weeks. We had owned the house for four years, and by the time we paid the fees, we came away with no cash.

We weren't going to walk away from our latest adventure without some help. We sold the business at a loss. Liz had a job working in the city. I was able to get $450 a week from employment insurance benefits, but things were really tight. Our families were there for us, but they had been down this road with us before, so they were reluctant to pass along very much cash. Our true friends remained there for us. They knew how hard Liz and I had worked. They knew how much we suffered. Without them this would have more horrific than it was.

My dad had offered us the family summer house outside of Halifax to live in until we got settled. It was ocean front. The 1,300 square feet was more than adequate other than the older part of the house was a bit chilly in the winter months but all the same, comfortable. I felt blessed we had this landing spot until we figured this thing out. Liz would only be an hour away from her family and when we had a job in the city our expenses would be low so we could get some cash flow and move to the city come spring.

This would be our place to do some soul-searching to get our lives back in order. I was slowly giving in to being humble. The last setback was a result of circumstances beyond my control. This one was a different story. We got squeezed by our circumstances, but what if we cut back and hung in there to make the last business work. I was giving in to taking ownership for this mess I created. Damn it was hard. What would I have to do to survive and provide for our family? The relentless desire to succeed still burned deep inside of me. The real task was to convince others I was worth the risk.

Liz and I took the time to figure out what to do with all the things collected over twenty years of marriage. The cottage was furnished, so we had all our belongings packed by professional movers and put into storage until we got settled. There were all the personal things we needed to take with us. Our closest friends were always there for us and when it came time to move they showed up with vans and trucks with trailers. I was grateful we had such friends and yet I was ashamed all at the same time. I was forty-five years old, penniless and jobless. We were like college kids on moving day. We were down to one car and a friend had come to the rescue with his ex-wife's old beater for me to drive. If you had told me ten years earlier that I would be going through this, I would have pushed you off the dock and not thrown you a life jacket.

Liz was working as a seamstress in the city and me out of work. We had a son in university in Quebec and another at boarding school. Thank god for the cash we put away for their education and the funds Liz's dad stashed away for them! Only a few knew the pain we were going through. Liz and I both had proud Lunenburg County German roots. It was instinctive, to not show your weakness. It all seemed a big lie. Come to think of it... it was.

During these many days alone, I started to take stock of my talents and how I could make my way in the world. I knew I could always sell. What could I do that would support an income I wanted and deserved? I spend a lot of time with a ruled pad with a line down the middle of the page going through the pros and cons of opportunities. I had even come to the notion that I would sell cars and that would be a great living. That, of course if I was selling high end cars to the crowd that wasn't calculating if they could afford the monthly payments. In the end, I felt I would not be happy in a car showroom weeknights and Saturdays. I learned as well that I was better suited to the business-to-business life than the business-to-consumer life.

I came to learn as well that most jobs never get posted in the newspaper or on job websites. In actual fact, only ten percent of them got posted. It amazed me that the people applying for these positions are actually wishing they get the job among hundreds of people that apply. If you want to get the job you want, you first have to know what you want. You must find a way to get the message out with laser precision. A lesson I learned from my insurance years was asking for referrals. I did not make direct asks to be hired. I would approach business leaders asking them for a moment of their time. I asked them for their expert advice on what would you do if you were me. Very few ever said no to seeing me. People generally want to help people. I used the notion that if they liked me and my skill set, they would automatically refer me to someone in their business network who was looking for a talent like mine. This way of approaching a job hunt like this builds a huge business network. It also shows you have the initiative and drive successful business owners want working for them. Having gone through this job hunting exercise a few times in my life, I can tell you that my business network is well over a thousand people.

The strange part about this time in my life is that my "Aha" moment didn't appear. I was so hoping it would but it failed to bop me on the head. Those moments came later in life, when I least expected them. It was more like an evolution derived from soul-searching and a lot of time on my hands. I wanted to do what brought me joy. What could I do to earn good money and most importantly, maintain my self-esteem? I struggled with my ADD, wanting everything here and now. Half of my earning career was over and I was flat broke. I knew I needed to suppress taking a job I didn't like and fail at it. That would be a death worse than my school years. I wrestled with my patience like never before. I knew the right thing was there for me, I just had to be patient. Proof once again that wisdom is truly earned.

The painful part of my soul-searching was feeling hopeless. You are dependent on others just to make ends meet. It is a very humbling experience to accept the help of others. If there is a word that best describes the situation, it is the feeling of extreme vulnerability. Your weaknesses are fully exposed. It comes to all those who are risk takers much like myself. If it doesn't work out, we become exposed. I now understand why so many people are risk averse. The unfortunate part is they become spectators in life and not participants.

I related my failures back to my goal setting. Chasing the big one million number had created a creature I didn't like or fully understand. These goals had let me down. It was all hocus pocus. I gave up goal writing, but the visions of grandeur never left my mind. I guess you could say I was still goal-orientated, but it didn't reside on a page in my book of goals any longer. I had closed the covers on that book, with no plans to open it again for a few years, until I discovered I had been doing it all wrong. I really had myself in a pickle.

All of these negative thoughts about goals racked around my mind with an uneasiness that sat like a lump of bad food in the pit of my stomach. What about all the things I learned in Ledgehill years earlier? What about all those days of introspection and figuring out the path I would take on my life journey? I wasn't feeling those emotions of bliss at this stage of my life. The relentless drive I possessed to prove to the world I am worth it became my guiding light. I would never allow myself to give up.

I had been out of work three times in my life, and I had strangely begun to enjoy them. They became a grounding exercise for the mind and the soul. I created a to-do list and stuck to it, and got a lot of exercise. It helped keep the brain fresh. Being a serial volunteer also allowed me to keep myself busy helping where I could in the community. It was a great way to network. Successful people give back. There are fewer, better places to get involved than in the community. The bonus is the people you meet. Giving pays off. I'm living proof.

Asking for the advice of successful people is a great exercise. Bright ideas and answers don't come out of thin air. They come after you ask a question. Chances are, many successful people have gone through hard times. Not everyone is born into a successful career. They paid a price somewhere along the line. The number one rule in sales is ask! Ask for the appointment and ask for their business. The same applies to getting where you need to go. Something as simple as the pros and cons exercise with yourself is really asking questions from my view. Bill, a great friend in the Rotary world, always used to say to his club with a cute play on words: "Get your ask in gear."

Being honest with yourself is critical to your success in any venture. Contrary to what some folks will tell you none of us are good at everything. Humans are strange creatures. We believe that if we tell ourselves something enough times, we start to believe it even if it isn't true. That is a nasty trap that's to be avoided. Perception is reality doesn't apply to self-analysis. It took me years to understand that I was great at building business, but lousy at running them. Running them is routine. Routine is boring. I'm an ADD. I like fast-paced action. Know your strengths and play to them. If you have a great idea for a business and you don't know how to promote or sell your great idea, it will die on the shelf. Put in the time and money to truly know your strengths.

An important part of being humble is taking your ego out of the decision making process. If you don't, it will cloud your judgement. Yes, it will rumble around in the back of your mind but stifle it. If you are unable to do that, go back to the pros and cons exercise. It will bring you back to reality. Great decisions come from a balance of being rational and listening to your gut.

Some folks are lucky and get their aha moment early in life. For me, it came from knowing what I wanted right from the get go just like a good student who knew early in life they would be a doctor. We are somehow wired for it. The challenge comes when we get knocked off the rails and we need to reinvent ourselves. These moments in our lives shape us to who we are. We begin to evolve through an exercise of necessity created by unplanned setbacks we are faced with. The gem in all of this is it makes us stronger. We truly do learn from our failures. I can tell you from experience I am long past sweating the small stuff. Drama is left for the stage and TV. It has no place in the business world.

Know when it's time to reinvent yourself.

The mother of invention didn't run a repair shop. When life gets tougher than pushing a soggy rope up a hill, it's time to get gravity working for you.

CHAPTER THIRTEEN

THE FIRST "AHA!"

Key Concept:
The reward is unconditional giving.

With age, one comes to realize the power of relationships. Networking is the best way to come across a great job. I got a call from a friend saying their computer supplies specialist was leaving the company, and was I interested. The job was not yet posted on a job board or website. The job was with the world's largest office supply company and it was to work with their twenty-three sales people they had in Eastern Canada. I could not believe my luck. It was a junior position that I would not have been looking for, but there was an opportunity to grow in big organizations. The pay was respectable, and this time I would be on the front edge of a technology wave and not the back side. I knew this was going to be a fun ride.

The company was managed by three brothers, who had recently sold out to Corporate Express and they had a contract to remain on to manage the business and continue to grow sales in Eastern Canada. I had known this family since I was ten. They hired me and I was off to the races. It was John, one of the brothers, whom I would be reporting to, and we were both real promoters and sales types. I actually went to the National Youth Sailing Championships in Ottawa with John decades before.

My role would be to introduce computer products and the huge opportunity it held for the traditional office product sales team who were selling traditional ruled pads, pens and file folders. The opportunity to lift sales volume excited the hell out of me. I knew I was on to something really good.

I have always been one to help, even offering assistance to those I compete against. Not to send them business, but help them get started. They had come into the office supply business a few years after me and we were not in the same trading area. I helped them find good suppliers and helped them understand who the players were. I was President of the Nova Scotia Office Products Association at that time and I knew all the suppliers and other independent players in the business. It was part of my role as President to help us all grow.

John would tell you today he hired me because I had helped him years before to get a solid footing with his business and he knew I would do a great job. It was a win-win! The foundation was based on trust coupled with a solid relationship. They also knew it would not take me long before I was up flying and helping grow the division. Deep down, I still loved the office products business even though I was now working for one of the big U.S. corporations who mowed me down and had forced me into bankruptcy eight years earlier. If you can't beat them, join them, as they say. My wife Elizabeth had also secured a great job in the Human Resource business about the same time. Things were looking up and we moved out of my parent's summer house two months after I started my new job. We moved into a great house back in Halifax, which has us closer to our many friends and family. Life was good.

Things were going very well. I couldn't believe my luck to be with a strong, successful company and a warehouse full of inventory to sell from. I just needed to focus growing sales and be in tune to new products as they came down the line. The company had built out a great sales team that was driven and eager to do well. There were the guys you worried about with poor results and having enough food in the fridge, but they were few. My computer products division was leading all other branches of the company across the country. I was being sought out by other product managers and sales leaders to find out how we were doing so well. I can't take all the credit, as I inherited a great sales team that bought into the new products and ran with it. Timing is a wonderful thing, especially when it happens to you.

This success had brought me into the inner circle of sales leaders across the company in both the US and Canada. I became part of several committees whose role it was to leverage new sales opportunities from within the existing customer base. It was a great boost to my ego and self-esteem after a few years of quite frankly rotten luck. Perhaps my lot in life is to be with a major corporation I thought.

The success of my division afforded me new opportunities within the company, and that meant I was getting lots of leadership training. I was heading off to courses here and there and I was also offered the opportunity to become a corporate trainer that had me hanging out with the VPs and other leaders in the company. On one such session I attended was in Orlando, Florida. It was a sales leader summit with an outstanding facilitator. As Tom led us, he held my attention for two straight days. He was amazing to learn from and so full of positive energy. Following the two-day event, I went up to Tom and said, "Thank you. You have held my attention for two straight days. Nobody can do that with me. I don't know what it is but thank you." Tom looked at me, smiled and said, "I'm an ADD." Bewildered, I responded, "So am I." He responded with, "Aren't we lucky? Let's go for a beer after I finish cleaning up."

The next hour was probably one of the most enlightening hours of my life. Tom said without a second thought. "Aren't we lucky to have all this intelligence? All this energy! All these interpersonal skills! The laser focus we ADD's have is awesome! All this love to give! We are blessed Paul." Hearing these words after years of trying to deal with the scourge of being ADD knocked me on my ass. A blessing! ADD. Really? After we finished the beer and kept stresing that I should embrace this blessing I began to cozy up to this notion that we are lucky. It's amazing what can happen when we look at life through a different lens. In my case this was a transformational moment in my life. I truly am lucky.

Once I got the hang of being lucky, I continued on my strategy of rapid sales growth and kept dreaming of climbing the corporate ladder. I was getting the attention of the very top brass and I was poised for success. I had been travelling to other branches presenting the Miller Heiman Consultative Selling Process the company had embraced. It was interesting to see in my travels who embraced these new concepts and I learned very quickly to read a room full of sales people. I knew the winners and the strugglers within fifteen minutes. Not only was I helping the sales teams become more effective, I was learning the process myself. I use this process today in all my sales-related activities. This concept is so spot on. I could not believe my luck to be sharing my knowledge and learning all at the same time. And getting paid for it.

I believed as well that my success was related to several things: the drive to succeed, fuelled by my ADD, along with my entrepreneurial approach to business. I was usually the first one in the office every day and one of the last ones to leave. Nothing trumps work ethic. This corporate world really opened my eyes as I visited some branches and it wasn't safe to stand near the front door at closing time. You were likely to get mowed down by the rush of the staff heading for the exits. I couldn't understand why they did not embrace this opportunity like I did.

I applied to be Divisional Vice President when the position became available and I came in second. This happens in corporate life and it deflated me to no end. I had knocked it over the fence which huge sales growth. As it turned out I had played my cards wrong with who I was supporting. I had reported to the new divisional President some questionable sales reporting that negatively impacted my division just a few months earlier. He ultimately had the last say in who was hired. I was offered a package just a few weeks following the loss and downsized out of the company. It was the strangest compliment a man can receive, to be offered close to a year's pay in settlement after just over two years of being employed. "You did an amazing job Paul. We are changing the way we run the division now." It was the strangest feeling of hurt and gratitude.

With big corporations comes internal politics and power struggles. It takes a lot of tact and nerves of steel to rise to the top and even then that can be a wobbly perch. My entrepreneurial spirit and drive fueled a rapid growth in sales and I was afforded opportunities. I learned a ton about myself and marketing. That being said, the entrepreneur in me created a similar outcome to my departure at the race track. When it comes right down to it, I love solving problems and creating solutions that drive my sales success. I do whatever I do with passion. I came away from this one with my head held high.

I have come to learn that I love flexibility in business life. The corporate world doesn't buy into the notion of flexibility as it's tough to measure. Corporations are answerable to their shareholders. It's usually about the money. If you're considering being part of a large company and want to have an impact you need to do your homework. I do believe that corporations can be very different depending on the corporate culture. That comes from the top and the leadership style. My entrepreneurial spirit is best suited for smaller organizations where flexibility allows change to take place quickly, unlike the etched in stone business and sales plans of the larger corporate world. I learned how to be adaptable to change the hard way. Not that I wasn't willing to embrace it more over understanding how quickly business trends change. Understanding how technology or market trends take place and evolve is tricky business. The old adage of spending time working on your business is step one to seeing what's coming down the pipe.

My experience in the corporate world was thrilling to say the least. I will never regret the opportunity I had to learn. To experience first hand how having the reserves, working capital and inventory will allow you to penetrate a new market was invaluable. I came away with problem solving skills that I had not used before. The key though is focus. We can't take our eye off the ball, or we lose market share. Be deliberate in your decisions while being nimble and adaptable to change. There are times when success is creating a different view of the same product the competition has. This different view can create a new demand and in some ways much similar to my outlook about ADD. Seeing it through a different lens changes everything. Always make an effort to look at it from the customers perceptive. It's often different than your own. They buy your stuff; you don't!

The best advice is to always have the big picture in clear view. There can be a lot going on around the corner that will sneak up on you when you least expect it. Seeing the problems as they arise is one thing, dealing with them promptly is equally as important. Owning and managing a business that is hinged on the success of one or two products is vulnerable to attack from competition as well as product obsolescence. This happened to me in the computer forms business. The new laser printer alternative meant having thousands of new competitors where I once had just a few. It can happen that fast.

It's great to know everything about your business. This doesn't, however, mean that you need to be good at everything in your business. Details can be looked after by administrators. I call them historians. I don't want to diminish the value of these people, but often they are not the visionaries in your business. That's your role or your business partner's skill. If you are selling widgets make sure you're not on the assembly line making widgets. That may be what you did to start your company, but I recommend you be the one with your head up planning future advancements as soon as you can. Learn how to sell. There is nothing worse than being a business owner who doesn't understand or like sales people and then try to manage them. That's a lesson in futility. Learn how to sell, if only for the short term. Besides, people want to deal and buy from the owner. It makes them feel more important. Now that's looking at things through a different lens.

The reward is unconditional giving.

The act of giving is win-win. If we gave expecting nothing in return, there is no reason to keep a score card. Just think of the time you will lose trying to keep track of you owe me one.

CHAPTER FOURTEEN

THE DARKEST TIME

Key Concept:
Resilience will always trump survival.

At forty-nine years of age I had handled many misfortunes in my life but it was starting to wear on me. How much more could I withstand before I fell apart? I had been coined a survivor. This is not what I would consider endearing. I had worked hard to be a somebody and it just wasn't working out so well. The weight of the world seemed to be squarely planted on my shoulders. It has been said we, baby boomers, will have three careers in our life. Holy *jumpin*, I was just forty-nine and on my ninth job in twenty years! They say when you're living in the past you are depressed. I can tell you it's true.

Challenges at work were creating challenges at home as well. My wife and I loved each other very much, however, we never really saw eye to eye on how to raise the boys and this was becoming evident with their performance in university and boarding school. Living the champagne life on a beer budget was not really a good atmosphere in which to raise a family. Appearances were important to Elizabeth and I was about making every effort to not to show what lay under the surface. The boys keep on living the good life and this added to the weight. I still had the nice income from my settlement after being downsized, but the self-esteem warning light was flashing on my dashboard.

I had an opportunity to go back into the insurance business and I took the insurance exam and passed with flying colors. The company specialized in accidental death and health insurance targeted at Union workers. There I was, once again backing the hearse up to the door, four nights a week trying to sell policies. It seemed easy enough, but the manager of the company was not a person whose leadership style I warmed up too. I quit after two months. This was the one time in my life my mother was right. She advised me not to do this. I ran the white flag up the pole the next time I saw her after I quit.

I managed to land a great job with a well managed local company in the contract furniture and photocopier business. Perhaps this would be my turning point. Unfortunately, they hired a guy who wasn't able to deliver on his A-game. The pressure to be a good father and a good provider also made it difficult to deliver on my promises. I always did, but those were stressful times which added to my mental discomfort. I fought off the deep feelings of failure and worried that I may slip into depression. I constantly asked my doctor father if this was the case, and in each instance I received a firm no.

One just can't live in a vacuum at home and expect to show up at work being an over the top producer and vice versa. It's all intertwined. My days became a routine and I was doing only what I had to do. What was to be gained from putting on the cape and tights like I did years ago? It didn't work so well then, and certainly it wouldn't work now. It became easy to beat myself up and start to make excuses. I was starting to slide into the blame game. I had never done that before in my life. I felt damn uncomfortable and certainly not myself; however stress causes us to do things in irrational ways. My Aha moment just a year earlier really hadn't taken hold. I was still trying to deal with my anxiety created from thoughts of being a total fuck-up.

To add to the discomfort, I never got the job I was hired to do and that bothered me. I felt cheated. It appeared to me they really wanted me for my expertise in the computer and printing products side of the business. I was happy to do that for a period as long as I got to where I wanted to be and was hired for. Deep down, I knew this was a symptom of feeling listless, undervalued and I was bringing all of this on myself. It was mentally debilitating and downright depressing.

I had asked several times about this with my direct report and he kept putting off the discussion. It was an uncomfortable conversation. I was living under the delusion that if I got the job I was hired to do all would be well. Looking back on this nothing could be further from the truth. I knew my performance was not good enough and I was standing on thin ice. I didn't push the issue ever again.

I made a hire who was a real star in the printing products business. I knew him from my days in the office supply business. If it was made Kevin knew where and what machines they were used in. He helped me get away from the detail stuff I didn't like. I knew he would allow me the time to go out and grow sales. Managing a few sales people along with my own production was invigorating, however two of these staff members left the company which took the polish off my abilities to manage and get the job done. Like the last job with corporate, I was downsized. In both cases, the great hires I made ended up with my job. There is a silver lining in my abilities, but the cloud wasn't big enough to float my worn out self-esteem. I guess I can chalk that up to it being business.

All this stress and life on the road out selling pushed me to alcohol. I have enjoyed a drink all my life. I saw my father come home from the hospital every day and settle in his lazy chair to enjoy a glass of gin and decompress. I too had picked up the habit. Booze didn't own me; however, my consumption was over the allowable limit in the Canadian Food guide! The one or two glasses of wine per evening had turned to consuming a whole bottle or more every evening. It became my companion. Wine was the juice that suppressed the shame I had brought upon myself and more importantly my family. Life certainly isn't always fair, and I unfortunately I seemed to attract more than my fair share of unrest.

The stress of endless job losses and disagreements on how to raise the boys was taking its toll. The boys were young men and were living a good life while we the parents had very little reserves to sustain this for much longer. Our backgrounds and parenting styles were totally different. I was from the old school where we raised our children to be good adults and to go after their dreams and goals. Once out of school, they would have the tools to make their own way. Liz's upbringing was similar but more in the we support them until they graduate from university camp. We ran out of money trying to support that notion. Both of us good parents, however, with very differing views. Who was I to argue with her point of view? I didn't have a university education and look at all the trouble I have got myself into. I was smart enough to know when to back down.

Both the boys had failed their first year at university. Let's just say they each single-handedly increased the share value of Labatt's Brewery by five percent. I was a party boy too when I was younger, so I swallowed my tongue. I suppose much like my father did with me when I was playing hooky in high school. The parallels are really quite profound. One of my sons got back on the educational track, while the other chose my route of carving his way in the business world. The biggest challenge was really for me as I worried about the conflicting messages coming from their partners. My parents played a larger role in my parenting ways, but they also had their differences. I wore my emotions on my sleeve, much like mom always wore the façade the all is well in the world, even though she was in turmoil under the surface. These mixed messaged from my parents messed with my own value system. Mom was constantly telling me how to live my life and when I would arrive home after such visits Liz would often say, "You visited your mom today didn't you?" "I can tell because you're all messed up."

The load of constant business distress and both of us not living the dream saw the end to a twenty-five-year marriage. I loved her so very much and I was riddled with guilt I had put her through this mess. I was amazed and grateful she stood by me for so long. We should never forget the importance of the work-life balance. I am so very grateful that our sons truly did get the best of both of us. Both with their mother's love of family and wonderful temperament. They inherited my drive, focus on success and a great work ethic. We did get some parts of this right.

The perfect storm hit me square in the heart. I was a mess. Failed businesses, jobs and now a failed marriage. I thought I would never end up divorced. Just add one more failure to the pile Paul! I missed all the tell tale signs. Perhaps if I ran away from all this I could get a fresh start. I had time on my side. I could still become a success. Little did I know that success can be measured in so many different ways. The future I hoped would define who I really am. I had reached a new low and there was nowhere else to go but up.

Life really all happens inside the blender. We can't just put certain parts of our lives in silos. They are all interconnected. Like it or not, if you have troubles at home, they show up at work and vice versa. Sweeping your problems under the carpet only delays the inevitable. We know they will come back to haunt us, but we do it anyway. Perhaps they are our own foolish ways of hiding from the truth! Let's face it. We all do it. That was the space I was in. I was running from myself. The weight of my past had been winning the war. We just have to remember that denial is not a river in Egypt.

Communicating with our partners is critical. We were doing that, but it was usually about problem solving business issues. Hindsight really is 20-20. It's being able to focus and openly discuss our emotions in the present that is the most important in all relationships personal and business. Expectations are what guide us. When they fall short, the train comes off the rails. I learned about myself from this experience and it's extremely tough to fend off regret, especially when I admitted I caused much of this distress. Life really hits you up side the head when 'that will never happen to me' does. I had never dreamed I would be divorced and now I am. We didn't learn this shit in school!

When life gets really dark like it did for me, it's easy to slide into bad habits like feeling sorry for ourselves. Wine became my friend in troubled times. It dulled the senses, but trying to suppress the truth is like circling the bowl. If we're not conscious of this, we will fall down the pipe from which the way back out is a huge climb. Push back the temptations to eat or drink your way out of your troubles. I am always reminded of my favorite author and blogger Seth Godin's line: "The best time to go for a walk is when we don't want to."

Don't allow yourself to be declared a survivor. It may speak to your toughness, but it really doesn't define that you have bounced back. It suggests that you're still in the ring fighting it out. Resilience is the appropriate word to best describe a recovery from any major setback. It speaks to your ability to learn from your failures and be a better person because of it. Blessings come to us in many ways, and they don't always seem fair or just. There is good in everything. I suggest you spend your time during those tough periods in your life looking for the blessing. Setbacks are often disguised as lessons.

Resilience will always trump survival.

Resilience is a trait that can be learned if it's not embedded in your DNA. There is a lot to be said about the value in believing you're worth it. There is no greater way to win admiration than to come back better and stronger than you were before.

CHAPTER SIXTEEN

IT GETS BETTER

Key Concept:
The dots will connect. Be patient.

After having been out of work a few times in my life, it became less intimidating to be out of work. It had worked out in the past, and I knew it would certainly work out in the future. You just know where to look and figure out what you're good at.

I was keeping myself busy at the marina and was a partner, however, that was an equity-building exercise. Deep down, I still wanted to be in business. If I was going to put any money away for later in my life I certainly wouldn't be able to do that on a modest salary over the next twenty years. The funny thing about being out of work it seems like everyone is out looking. It's like the feeling you get shortly after buying a new car. You see an endless supply of the same color blue cars that you have. What's with that? To be in your fifties and out looking for work becomes a struggle to be unique. What is it that will help you stand out from the crowd? Various offers to work come in from friends and companies who want you to start on straight commission without even a float or base salary. These fools actually think they are doing you a favor. If there was ever a case that it's all about me, this was it.

The job market is full of fifty-somethings who have been recently downsized in the efforts of the corporate world to bolster up the bottom lines. I saw this as a Wall Street shareholder driven way to dump high paid middle managers and squeeze them out of future pension income. Spineless bastards! The lives and families of millions of North American have been destroyed by corporate greed. I must be honest and say that working for a smaller family owned business where you are valued as a person and not just a dollar bill is the preferred place to land. Just like the blue car the fifty-somethings are everywhere out looking for work. The baby boomers appeared to be a bust. The challenge for these displaced workers was to calculate what their real value was in the work place.

I was reading Canada's national newspaper, *The Globe and Mail*, when I saw an article for an upstart company called Prime 50. The founder was interviewed and the whole thing made sense to me. The business was to be based on helping downsized fifty-somethings find meaningful work. This was at a time when internet job boards like Monster were all the rage. The Prime 50 businesses are aimed at helping out of work boomers find work. I had trouble controlling my excitement at the opportunity and it was time to do my due diligence.

One thing I had learned from the past was not to ask just your friends what they thought as they would give you their emotional opinion and just not one based on reason. I asked business leaders and headhunters what they thought. It was thumbs up everywhere. I would never go out and rush into this so I did my usual pro and cons exercise with a line down the middle of the page. This is a real gut test not to be ignored.

The price for the franchise seemed reasonable, and I was off to Toronto to meet with the franchisor and other potential franchises. The franchisor was a very successful Chartered Accountant in Toronto, and I felt that if a CA didn't have this figured out, who would? The other potential franchises were just as enthusiastic as me to get started. I pulled out my check book and officially acquired the franchise for Nova Scotia. I dreamed of really knocking this one over the fence. I was a serial entrepreneur if there ever was one.

The operating costs were manageable starting out as a home-based business. I paid a monthly fee to the parent company to list available jobs on their web site. All I had to do was go out and find the jobs to list. I was a sales whiz so this would not be that tall of an order. This idea was so leading edge it was easy to get radio and newspaper interviews. I was able to get huge exposure for the company without high advertising bills. The message hit a nerve with the prime readership base of the local newspapers. The excitement was mounting. My phone and email inbox was full of messages from the fifty-something job seekers within days of the word getting out. Holy jumping this is going to be fun, I thought.

The key was for me to hit the streets and get in front of the decision makers and tell them about my stable full of great people ready to work for them. These people were highly motivated. They want to work and they certainly don't need to be managed. These boomers brought a skill set so there is less training involved. They were also willing to work part time and on contract.

The high costs of hiring are well-known in today's business world. Hiring from my stable could save those costs over the long haul because they will stay unlike the fickle Generation-X types moving from job to job very quickly. It all seemed so logical until I started to run into the Gen X Human Resource staff who could not buy into the value proposition of hiring a pro at less than you would think.

All the while, my phone was ringing off the hook from job seekers who saw me as the second coming of Christ. The stories they would tell me of the unfairness of the system they built was a daily song playing in my ear. It seemed I was headlong into the face of the decision makers who let them go. I hadn't calculated that in my due diligence. I wasn't alone. My counterparts across the country were experiencing the same thing. Within six short months the fan fair was over. The franchisor had lost a small fortune and sold the name to a big player in the HR world. I was left being owed commissions and a very weak offer from the company that bought the rights to Prime 50. The job interview was with a team of three Generation X types. I couldn't get out of the room fast enough knowing working for these folks was not cut out for me. Good people, but not for me.

There was, however a silver lining. While I was out knocking on doors trying to sell Prime 50, I was getting opportunities to go and work for some pretty good companies. Don't ever underestimate doing a good job as you will attract other jobs. I took a contract with a marine supply company that was an absolute blast. I knew and respected the owner. What could be more fun than being in the marine business selling to boat builders and fishing supply companies? It was a long way from being President of a fast growing company, but I was having fun.

The lesson from the Prime 50 escapade was the customer's perception is reality. This is a Dale Carnegie teaching that will never go out of style. His teachings are timeless. The Prime 50 concept was a genius idea. Who would not have believed that hiring talent at a lower cost than they used to work for would have failed? Mind boggling! This would make sense in any business model. Myself and a whole lot of other people were completely caught off guard. In my business life today, I spend more time focusing on the customer's needs and perceptions than I do with any of the details. Folks don't buy details. They buy what they believe. It's that simple.

The whole package is important. There is a space for generalists in the business arena. When was the last time you heard of a General Manager? Many are disguised as entrepreneurs. That was me. My business mind has found a nice balance of reason and really getting to know where my talents lie. Life is so much better now. I have swallowed a lot of pills over the years that haven't tasted so good. The old adage of that didn't taste so good really holds true. I couldn't wait to wake in the mornings and go make my way. I was newly married to a successful woman and life was really refreshing. Stella brought a great energy to my life and I was grateful to have her support while I got my life in order.

I went through a lot of years without liking myself – years of beating myself up, questioning if I was worthy of success played heavily on my mind. It all seemed a lie. How could I really hold my head high after so many business failures? My wife and others questioned me, why would you go and get a coaching designation when you have had so much failure in your past. Those statements hurt, but I pushed past them as the one thing I had gained was wisdom. Wisdom is really gained on the front lines of life. I showed empathy for those who struggle and have struggled. There is a lot to be said for having walked in your shoes. I brought to the coaching arena the 'been there, done that,' which in my view brought me credibility. Not the other way around. I had lived first-hand what my coaching clients were going through. People don't naturally leap from one success to another. I find peace in knowing more headwinds will come my way, but those head winds are there to validate the direction I am headed.

My new marriage brought many new connections that were leading me to new relations both personal and business. Life wasn't a picnic; however, there was much to be said for freshness. I expect this is why I have always embraced change even when it has not seemed fair. I had given in to the notion my past had created someone I really liked. The school of hard knocks can be handled in many different ways. We can lie down, beaten or we can walk through life showing our scars for all to see. The badge of courage! That has a nice ring to it.

The customer is king! The customer is the only decision maker when it comes to moving a deal along. We can choose not to play that game, but I caution against that. There are ways to give the customer what they want, but we can define the terms. That's our control. There is much to be said for saying "no" to a potential customer. If we sell them using old fashioned sales tactics, they will have remorse and the deal will come back to bite you. I am forever being thanked for explaining how it all works. I'm all for transparency. If we have done our job and given the buyer all the right reasons to buy, we have a long-term customer. They made a buying decision. These types of customers provide referrals. These types of customers will come back again and again. It's all based on trust.

Life is really about balance. We will all face some shit storms in our lives and we would be foolhardy to think they won't happen. It's critical we are honest with our employers and our spouses. We have all heard stories of people leaving the house to go to work at a job they don't have, all because they are afraid to tell their spouse. How often have you put off letting an underperforming employee go? We labor over these decisions for what could be months and months only to breathe a sigh of relief when it's done. Life really could not have seemed to get any worse. The reality is that when we face our fears head on the storm passes much sooner. The weight of the decisions removed from our thoughts allows us to focus on new opportunities and life in general becomes a better place both at work and at home.

When we try to connect the dots too soon we miss the chance to perhaps move the dot as it was in the wrong place. This can lead us down the wrong road. Allowing things to evolve before we connect the dots is sage advice to me. It became very evident to me that the connections I made in my past are the connections that open new doors. The person opening the door might be a direct contact or it will come from referrals that took place as a result of connecting with people. Dots can move just like people move. Be adaptable. Be open and give of yourself. Most importantly, be your authentic self.

The dots will connect. Be patient.

Like a ship's navigator we head toward targets or dots on the chart. Each dot is an achievement that links us to our destination. Like life, an ocean passage is about the journey. The stormy days mixed with brilliant sunshine mold us to who we are today. Captains of our own destiny!

CHAPTER SIXTEEN

LEAVING LAND

Key Concept:
Make ideas float.

Opportunities come to us in strange ways every now and then. A close American sailing friend was looking to make an investment in Nova Scotia, where his family has summered for three generations. I had known Topher for close to ten years, and I had sailed with him and his family on their yacht in Chester for many years. Toper got caught in a power play squeeze with his employer and got shown the door. Senior VPs of a worldwide corporation don't get pushed out the door without some do-ray-me. He had a yachting facility on his mind as a place to invest some capital. He asked me if I would be interested. We both had deep roots in the yachting community and it seemed a natural. He wanted my help to build the business into a desired yachting facility on the south shore of Nova Scotia.

I was recently divorced. I had time on my hands, plus a good job, so I wasn't in need of a pay cheque out of the business. The romance of being in the boat business was a dream come true. I needed to figure out a way to be accessible to the business yet be fair to my employer. I had been renting a house on the water in St Margaret's Bay and it was a quick thirty-minute drive to Chester. I had chosen the house in the Bay to live, as I wanted to live on the water from here out in my life.

My banker Steve had said to me, "Paul, you would find a way to live on the water even if it meant living in a tent." He wasn't far off with that statement.

Being short on cash and anxious to be back in business, I accepted based on being provided an equity position with options for each year of growth. Topher had also asked another local business man to be the treasurer and the man with the local contacts. It seemed a no brainer and a great way to build some equity and be in the boat business. I felt the business had great growth opportunities as it had lacked investment in the property or a sales plan by the previous owners. In fact, the owner bought it as a real estate play out of a bankruptcy eight years earlier. The land was okay, but a bit hilly for boat storage but doable. The water lot was just fair as it was not a deep water facility. This brought challenges to renting marinas to larger yachts. The optimist in me still saw opportunity.

I accepted and became the president and a minority shareholder. My nights and weekends for the next two years were now deeply entrenched in Gold River Marina. I loved it so much I moved to Chester to be closer to the facility. Good fortune seemed to be coming my way. Forget the fact they roll up the sidewalks in November for the winter, there I was, a single guy forty-nine years young.

This was my second go at being in a business partnership. There was a multitude of expectations of each of the partners. This became a challenge from time to time. I was doing my part, calling existing customers assuring them that we, the new owners, were going to give the facility a facelift. We would continued to be a facility they would be proud of. I was also working very hard bringing in new customers through my many contacts. The facility had a bad name in the yachting community due to its rocky past and lack of investment. It was my job to turn that all around. My partner Leigh was real strong on the administrative side, and a stickler for details. He was also a control freak, which didn't sit that well with the cut of my jib but he was certainly a great asset to the business. I swallowed my tongue more than enough times those first couple of years. I knew the business would never be big enough to be my retirement plan, but I felt it could certainly add to it.

I was having fun and it didn't take me long to get a good grip on the ideal customer. Being a sailor was where my passion lay, but I learned that many of the best customers were the power boaters. Wind is free! A sailor will always sail if they can go as fast as the engine can push them. The average sailboat owner might spend in whole year what a power boater might spend on fuel on a weekend. The bulk of the complaints when the haul out bill arrived were the sail boat owners. In fairness, there were many great sailboat customers who never batted an eye at the bill. It just seemed strange to me the successful power boaters just said fill her up and give her a good wash and never batted an eye when they got the bill.

I landed another job in the city that demanded my time seven days a week as well as a new romance that had me spending more time in the city. I had started to drift away from the business. As much as I loved doing what I was doing, I didn't see a logical financial return for my investment of time. The business was growing and profitable, but it needed an infusion of cash to upgrade the facility to attract a higher level of customer. I had come to the conclusion that it would be a very long time before I would reap any financial benefit, and yet so many hours of work still needed to be done. The three of us were at a different place as to where we should go with the business.

I did not have an exit strategy so I needed to create one. The needle of the compass was pointing in another direction for me and I became anxious to get out of the partnership. It made the most sense that our treasurer Leigh would purchase my shares so he would have a bigger stake in the facility. I was anxious to move on and he made me an offer that I would accept. He got a bargain, and in the big picture I came out of it okay.

I learned a lot from this experience, and it kept my entrepreneurial spirit alive. We came away friends, which is also important in the big scheme of things. Life just isn't about money. I took a big leap of faith that this would help me get back on track from a business ownership perspective. I might have been president but there were more cogs in the wheel just as important as mine. This business really needed good fiscal management to make it work. Marinas and boat yards have environmental issues that make bankers nervous. Banks won't lend money without a clear environmental certificate on the property. Liabilities can become expensive as we found out with a leaking buried underground fuel tank. During the environmental assessment, they found high levels of arsenic. They did feel a bit foolish when they discovered the water in front of the property was called Gold River. Of course, there were high levels of arsenic; they used to mine gold upstream.

If you're considering becoming an entrepreneur you must also surrender to the fact you don't make an hourly wage. As owners you're paid last, and sometimes paid nothing, while you build your business. I reached into my pocket numerous times over the years to help make payroll so the staff could be paid. It's the sacrifice you make as a business owner as you build your business. The rewards often come later when the business matures. If you want to be a successful entrepreneur, you had best embrace delayed gratification. The average person on the street has no concept of what it takes to be a successful business owner and the risks they take to be successful. Marriage mortality is also high among entrepreneurs as I learned, especially if your spouse has a regular paying day job.

I was involved in building a business which I loved with two great business partners. As they say, find your passion and figure out a way to make money at it. I was certainly living out my passion. The business was too young for me to realize any sort of regular revenue. When I would close down the gas bar and lock the doors in the evening I would hop in the boat and go for a spin around the bay. How many jobs does one get to do that with? Chester was like living in a postcard for five months a year. I had been hanging out with sailors all my life and this gave me the opportunity to work and play at the same time. It did spread me thin from a work perspective, but I was single and keeping busy hid my anguish from past business and personal failures low key, as I heard the money clock ticking. It was time to move on. I sold my shares two years later.

A business partnership can be like a marriage. When you think about it, it's very possible you would spend more time with your business partner than with your spouse. It was actually easier to have Liz as my business partner in the office products business as we complemented each other. It allowed us time to juggle the kids and was in fact a great way to raise our kids. They learned at an early age what work ethic is all about. Unlike a marriage, a business partnership should really have a finite life span. Figuring out the life span is a feat all unto itself.

The key to a successful business partnership is to know everyone's expectations. Everything from the growth plan, to how much time do you take for vacations and remuneration are all to be considered. What decisions can each partner make autonomously and what decisions are made by consultation with each partner. Many successful business people in business partnerships will tell you they are fantastic as each partner brings a different skill set which inevitably builds a stronger business. There is a huge emphasis on trust. You have to not micro-manage each other. It's always better to be inside the tent pissing out than outside the tent pissing in! You have to park your ego and consider the advantages. With partnerships you get to spread the risk and play on each other's strengths. Just have those parameters defined right from the get go.

Business types often forget one important thing when getting a business started. What's your exit strategy? We all don't live forever, and many of us don't want to work this hard all our lives. That being said, entrepreneurs usually work until they can't anymore, mainly because they love work. They love to grow business. All this being considered, you still need an exit strategy. If it's a partnership will there be enough cash on hand for the partner to buy you out? Is it an earn-out from an employee which is often a great plan as you will get some cash up front and draw a salary while semi-retired? Very few businesses are bought with cash. Today's tax system can rob you of your hard earned cash if you don't have an exit strategy. Shotgun clause for partnerships gone wrong are a topic all unto itself. Plan, plan, plan!

The term sweat equity means working for little or no pay while you build the business. My clause at Gold River had time served attached to share value. There will be sacrifices. Long working days and weekends are the norm. Putting off vacations is hard, especially when you have kids. One of the best accountants I had over the years advised me the benefits of ownership should be considered as rewards when benchmarks and targets are achieved. You have to plan them, as burnout can be your nemesis. I have suffered from burnout many times in my life, and when you're burnt out your decision making process can get all out of whack. Have a plan and stick to it. The most redeeming thing you can do for your business is make it attractive enough that someone wants to buy it. Bankers call it retained earnings. If you have those you will have a banking friend for life.

Make ideas float.

Floating an idea is really a buoyancy test. The detractors are trying to pull you under while you hastily fill the cracks to ensure the ship stays afloat. Once you have it right, you don't need to bail anymore.

CHAPTER SEVENTEEN

DEALING WITH MOM

Key Concept:
Your aha moment is coming!

The best meaning advice from around you is not always the best advice. Unsolicited advice is often worse. People close to you are often afraid to tell you the truth for fear of hurting your feelings or even worse hurt your feelings and not know they have done it. It's also easy to pass off this advice as cheap because we know the source. How often have you heard he would be great in sales? He is a real talker. My experience tells me the opposite. The best sales people are often the best listeners and those who say the least hear the opportunities. They are less threatening. I have learned the best advice comes from those who look at situations objectively.

My past failure had been weighing on me much of the last twelve years. I had always gone to the pros when I needed help. That being said, there is a never ending supply of free advice. Conversations that have 'your problem is' in them become very hurtful. Those who say it are out and out judgemental. To throw salt in the wound 'your problem is' is often unsolicited advice. These people just barge into your mind space and they have no idea the hurt they are causing. They foolishly think they are doing you a favour. When you have a few warts on you like I do some days standing naked on the street corner would be easier. I have learned to filter much of the unasked for advice over time. I now take it as just background noise.

Good meaning people sometimes do what they think is best for them in their advice for you, but they are not us. One size does not fit all. The best recipe for success is self-discipline. The armchair quarterbacks of this world are everywhere. Sports stadiums are full of them just like the halls of business. When it comes right down to it, they are spectators and not players. The world embraced the number one best-selling book *The Secret*, and they saw it as the silver bullet to getting what they desired. The book is only half right. It failed miserably to tell the readers you have to get off your ass and go out and do it soon after you put the image on your mind. The only silver bullet I know comes in a beer can.

I knew that my relationship with money was a real problem for me. Money ebbed and flowed and I wanted to wrestle with this once and for all. I met this gentleman at a networking event. There were twelve of us at the table and he stood out miles above the crowd. I knew I wanted to get to know this person better. He was insightful and he didn't have to say he was. It just radiated from him. I knew right then he was the person that could help unlock the money mystery for me. I hired Peter to be my coach. He would have full permission to pull out of me what he could. Those of us with experience know the answers are not always in plain view for us to see. We spent three sessions going through some steps and it was in our fourth session he said to me, "You will not get past this relationship with money until you deal with your mother. The relationship with your mother is the problem." Gulp!

You see, my mother had been telling me all these years that I was worth nothing until I made my money on my own. My mother was an endless supply of advice. Her unsolicited advice flowed like a river and it cut through me like a razor sharp knife. For fifty-four years, she had been finishing sentences for me. Mom was relentless in telling me how to live my life; and what to say, when, and where. You see, my mother never worked a day in her life when she graduated from finishing school. She inherited some money that she managed wisely, of which I am the benefactor of today, however it flew in the face of what she was telling me. Coach Peter had it right.

I finally got up the nerve to go and see my mother and have a conversation I should have had with her twenty-five years ago. When I arrived at the house I asked mom if she could come into the den so we could have a conversation. I said, "Mom, you have been telling me how to live my life. It has to stop." I touched my head and then my heart followed by, "There will be no more barging in here without my permission. If you feel that you have to tell me something, you must ask my permission. I would be more than pleased to listen." Well Christ, the waterworks were flowing from her eyes and she shook uncontrollably. I have to say my eyes were damp too. My heart was pounding like a jackhammer. I kissed her on her forehead and went out the door.

A few days passed and I decided to swing by the house like I normally would every week. My parents were in their mid 80s and ten-minute visits became an hour, as I was asked to help with this and that. Not a word was said by my mother about our conversation four days earlier. Not one bit of unsolicited advice. She smiled and hugged me. Something she rarely did. Over the following months she became my biggest supporter. Even when she moved to the nursing home, she had a big picture of me on her walker and would tell all who would listen who I was and how wonderful I was. So many years of heartache could have been avoided if we just had that conversation twenty-five years ago.

I learned a great deal from this and that we sometimes have to deal with the sticky stuff head on. When my parents died, there was nothing left unsaid. The experience, coupled with other difficult conversations, really helped me become a better business coach. I lived much of what my clients were struggling with. It gave me empathy, but also allowed me to help them find the courage to deal with the personal problems associated with their business. Many new businesses are funded by family members and when businesses start to fail the ones who helped you get started are usually the last to know when the shit hits the fan. I would help them deal with the rough stuff so they could move on and make better business decisions without the weight of disappointment on their shoulders.

A good coach helps their clients find their solution from within. I have gone for professional help many times in my life and I have never been disappointed. By some strange coincidence, I came by all this naturally. I was willing to peel a layer off of the onion to try and figure out how this energetic ADD me could harness the blessings that come from this syndrome. I was fully embracing those words from Tom a few years earlier. Aren't we lucky!

Not only did having the conversation with mom solve a personal problem, but it left me with a skill. I learned when we lean into the emotional fear and deal with the sticky stuff head on, the sooner we will be able to move on. Think of the times when you struggled over letting an employee go or when you came clean with your family about a skeleton in the closet. The weight is instantly lifted from your shoulders and often followed by a wish that we had done this earlier. Deep down, we know it, but it's the hardest thing we will ever do in our lives. I take great pleasure in helping people move on from these fearful situations. There were people there who helped me when I was at my lowest and now it's my turn to lift others out of their pain. I am blessed to know I have this gift, albeit earned in the trenches of life.

Often the issues are very plain for me to see when I am working with a client. Telling the client what the problem is won't help them in most cases. They don't have ownership if I tell them. The role of a coach is to lead your client down a road of self-discovery. This is accomplished by asking skilled questions. Their aha moment is much more impactful when it's them who turns on the light. The answer is inside them. I have felt liberated after a meaningful session with the coaches I have hired in the past. I work very hard to ensure they have that same feeling. Coaches like me who have the, been there, done that, can add that special sauce in their quest of the recipe of success.

Much of what we learn in life comes from what I call the slow drip. Those of us who have children know this. We as parents stay true to our message and eventually our children get it. Harry Chapin's song, *The Cat's in The Cradle* pretty much sums up the slow drip. "My boy was just like me." My sons learned the language of business at our kitchen table. I so remember the days that my boys 'got it.' If we watch closely enough, we can see the day they transform. They move on from being nocturnal creatures who, when they finally got out of bed at noon, then spent an hour in the shower, somehow change. Then one day they are up early and out the door to carve out a living and not complaining about it. Aha moments can happen at any time. Be aware. Watch and listen for them.

To really advance in this world we have to see the world view. We must constantly be honing our skills. Life is like golf. We keep going back because we want to be better. I recommend you take the same attitude with your life. Be prepared to spend money on improving yourself. I have spent tens of thousands on me over the years and I have never regretted spending it. The cost may seem a lot at the time, however in the big picture it's small. Consider what the average university student spends on getting an education with no guarantee of a job when they graduate. University doesn't prepare you for life. It provides you with a skill set for which to go forth in the world and make a living. Both of my sons are hugely successful in all aspects of their lives including business. I so remember the day my eldest son told me in his final year at university he just quit. No Shit! I said, "It's okay dad. I get it. I'll be fine. You didn't go to university and you have done well." Boink! I had no response. He was right. My parents had it right too when they taught us to be the person first. The rest will fall into place.

The best advice is the advice you pay for. You go into it expecting results. That's half the game. We must be open to letting our inner fears or disbeliefs be exposed if it's only between you and your coach. The leaders of industry and finance often use coaches to ensure they are performing at their best. They know their industry segment better than anyone but it doesn't mean they don't have any head trash that needs to be dealt with. The little bird that keeps chirping on your shoulder needs to be silenced. If coaching could be summed up in one word, it would be *clarity*.

We must deal with the sticky stuff as soon as we can. It's like your car when you're towing a trailer. It doesn't have the same get up and go. The baggage we carry around with us has the same effect. It slows us down. When is the last time you heard someone tell you that they told their family their problem and they threw them out the door? I suggest rarely, if ever. They will be disappointed, but odds are they love you more than you can imagine. They want you to be happy and to succeed. If you approach the sticky stuff with that notion, you are the odds on favorite to come out feeling relieved. I recall telling a friend the difficult story about the day I told my mother she wasn't allowed to barge into my heart and my mind. My friend, simply replied, "She just needed to know you were okay." Want an aha? I can tell you these moments are floating around out there. Just put up your antenna.

Your "Aha" moment is coming.

Aha moments always show up at the right time. Come to think of it, they can't ever show up at the wrong time.

CHAPTER EIGHTEEN

IT HAPPENED ON PURPOSE

Key Concept:
Strive to continuously improve.

I was sitting in a seaside cabin with my second wife Stella at White Point Beach Resort relaxing and having a glass of wine, cruising through the channels on the television, when I stopped at the PBS channel. I recall Jack Canfield speaking as one of the co-authors of the multi-million copy selling book, *Chicken Soup for the Soul*. I became intrigued and began to watch. He was talking about goal-setting and living out your dreams. I still had dreams, however, I had given up on writing goals a few years earlier. By some chance of fate, I continued to watch. Jack was so soft spoken and believable, I began to take notes. Never at any point did I feel like he was trying to sell me anything.

Mr. Canfield was explaining his recipe for success. "A recipe," I thought? Now this got my attention. His book, *The Success Principals*, had all the guidelines to follow. Most of the chapters had homework to ensure you were doing it right. The book touched on many topics like how to write your goals so they had more impact. He brought to our attention things like emulating and modeling yourself after successful people. Start preparing for the future by acting like you were already there, he said. It didn't appear to be hocus-pocus to me at all. It was becoming blatantly obvious I just needed to change the mix for my recipe to achieve success. Success was something that had come and gone for me numerous times in my life. I was seen in the eyes of others as being hugely successful. That, however, wasn't the guy I saw in the mirror each morning. I was suffering from a lack of self-esteem from all my previous struggles in life.

Mr. Canfield discussed that goals don't always have to be about money or material things. One point he did make very clear is that you can't include other people as part of achieving your goals. You can have a goal about how you will treat others and what you will do for them. He was emphatic that we break our goals down into bite size bits. Goals had to be stepping stones toward a larger plan. It was very obvious to me now the $1,000,000 goal had years earlier was missing some stages along the way. The clincher for me was when he said that people who write down their goals and actively review them are seventy-five percent more likely to succeed in achieving their goals than those who don't write them down. I was like a deer in the headlights, mesmerized by what I was watching before me.

The hook was set and I wasn't trying to wiggle off the hook. I was starting to buy into this goal setting business in a big way. I started to imagine all the things I could accomplish. It was an early fall evening and I went out on the porch when the show was over to reflect and listen to the roar of the ocean as there was a large surf running that evening. When I wasn't on the water, being at the ocean's edge is the next best thing. Nothing gets in the way of your view. It's always about the horizon. The possibilities of my future seemed endless.

During the show Mr. Canfield suggested we write down one-hundred things we wanted in our lives. I lit the fire to take the evening dampness off and I started to write down everything that came to mind. When you write them down, goals and aspirations can come up on your list pretty quick. My list was filled with places where I wanted to go. I was amazed actually to have made such a transitional change in my mindset in such a short period of time. I didn't doubt for one minute the exercise I just completed.

The following morning, while drinking my coffee, I read my list. How is it possible to have such a long list of things I wanted in life? They surely all wouldn't be achievable. As I was reading the list, I noticed that my wellbeing had made its way on to the list. My list wasn't all about money and assets. I was feeling this sense of contentment and calm that I hadn't not had for a very long time.

When I returned to the city on Monday, I rushed out and purchased the book. Stella did the same. I dove into the book like a child splashing in the beach water on a warm summer day. I had set out on a new journey – the journey of finding myself! Every time I had gone looking for myself in the past, I got lost. Surely, inside the covers of this book was the road map to my future success. Each chapter was a step with homework. I was scribbling notes on the side of the pages and highlighting the juicy stuff. There is so much in this book one can't possibly rush through it like it was a rainy weekend novel.

Every now and then, I would come across a chapter I wasn't ready for. Sticky gooey stuff that I skimmed over for a later visit. We are all guilty of doing this in our lives. I'm not a procrastinator, and somehow I didn't feel that as there was so much low hanging fruit in this book that I tackled the easy stuff first. I thought this approach would give me the quick results to get me cruising along, and for the most part it did. I could return to the tough stuff later. As it turned out it, a couple of years later I returned to do some of the chapter's homework for some areas of my life with which I struggled. Wanting things that make us feel good is easy. It's the 'why' that's hard. The need for validation with our goals and dreams can be a struggle for many of us.

While going through the book for the third time, I was ready to deal with my life purpose. Mr. Canfield was emphatic that you will not find real success until you know and understand your life purpose. Shit, you have to be kidding me. We get up. We enjoy our job. We love our family. We give back to the world as thanks for all we have. Frankly, it's really not that simple. Where does one begin?

During the following two months, I spent an inordinate amount of time pondering. I started to write the two sentences that would define who I am. I can tell you I had more shuffle and re-deals than a Las Vegas seven-card stud dealer. Just like a game of stud, it's the cards in the hole that only you can see that determine if you win the hand or not. Yes, one needs to bluff to win a hand of cards from time to time. It is not, however, something we should embrace when dealing with who we are. Bluff and fluff is not a credibility-building exercise.

I knew I didn't have it right. I dove into the internet and started to read about purpose. That word strangely made its way into the title of this book. I knew I was close, so I kept pressing on. My purpose couldn't be solely about my desires and goals. When you think about it a personal purpose can be something like a mission statement for a business. Don't get too hung up on that notion as I expect that ninety-five percent of employees don't know what their company's mission statement is. A mission statement likely created by a few of the executives on a weekend retreat. Personal purpose is not top down. It's your inside coming out. The common thread from my research was if we approach our projects and our relationships with purpose it has more meaning. It attaches emotion to the process and increases our chance of success.

In the weeks following, my revelation regarding purpose started to solidify. I knew I had to suppress my ADD tendencies to rush closure. I knew I must trust the process. I was very cognizant of the fact I could not hurry up this pivotal part of my life. In the big picture, taking a few extra weeks or even months to fine tune the missing piece to the puzzle was nothing. Going through this process confirmed to me Mr. Canfield' s decree that personal purpose is the key to a happy and prosperous life.

The best answers in life are the ones we have to dig for and not the ones in plain view. Much like a good coaching exercise, there are times when we peel back the layers to find the nugget within. They are often the most meaningful self-discoveries. Life isn't like the kids in the back seat asking 'Are we there yet?' We live in a world of instant gratification when the real joy lies with delayed gratification. We can thank advertising for the 'I want it now' generation. Instant gratification often has payments attached. I love Mark Twain's quote: "Why do people spend money they haven't earned yet to impress people they don't like?"

Stress or distress often keeps us up at night. Yumming down a bowl of Corn Flakes and watching television during the wee hours of the morning becomes habit forming when we are scratching for answers. Google might claim they have them, but they don't. They just have the rights to the search part. It's what happens when you click on the link that matters. We usually end up watching a show on how to become rich buying real estate with no money down. Yes, even the famous Tony Robbins can be found at 2:00a.m. while channel surfing. Make no mistake about this. Both of these two very different types of success get peddled while we are most vulnerable during a sleepless night. What they say is true. Only five percent of audiences will actually take the materials and act on it. They sit in boxes covered in dust some never having been open. I used to wear that badge and it's not the badge of honor. I don't turn on the television after 10:00p.m. any more. I have no need to. When I have insomnia, I get up and write an article, or I read. The mind is a magnificent muscle. I like to exercise mine regularly.

The famed Harvard School of Business says, "They will give you the tools needed to succeed. If you fail, it's your fault." No truer words can be said. Inaction is a disease that eats away at our self-worth. Stepping off the curb on a busy street takes guts. Taking the time to understand yourself so you can improve takes guts too. There are those among us who genuinely suffer from low self-esteem as a result of things that have happened in their past. Get some help. You're worth it. To the other ninety-five percent, you must decide that you have been a spectator far too long in this life. Get up off the couch and find another way to stimulate your imagination.

I am so grateful to be blessed with the desire to be always improving. It took a long time to figure myself out and just as long a time to like myself. Life was no longer a mystery. One of the one-hundred things on my list of goals from that night was to meet Jack Canfield in person. That goal came true in December of 2015. Jack was at a convention I was attending and of course he was signing his books that were available. I stood in line and waited. When it was my turn, I had my tattered old edition that was dog eared with post it notes protruding from the pages. I looked at Jack with my damp eyes and said, "Thank you." I asked Jack if he would sign this old edition that has been my road map the last ten years. We had a wonderful conversation that will stay with me until the day I die. It was Jack that helped me find my personal purpose.

Strive to continuously improve.

"My personal purpose is to be a role model of giving, love, wisdom, credibility, personal satisfaction, learning, happiness and joy that will inspire my family, friends, customers and associates."

CHAPTER NINETEEN

PIVOTAL BOOKS

Key Concept:
Provide great value.

I was cruising through the posts on LinkedIn one morning when I saw a banner. It was one where they make a special offer targeted to you based on your demographic. Bloody Google knows everything. This one that caught my attention. It said free download: "The Science of Getting Rich." I thought to myself. There is a science to this? I thought that stuff was for the Church of Scientology. I do have an inquisitive mind, so of course, I downloaded the book expecting I would have to make multiple clicks and leave my name dotted all over the internet however that was not the case. It took me right there.

It was a PDF version of the book and I printed it off for a Sunday afternoon read. It was a quick 120 pages. The author was Wallace Wattles, a Methodist Minister who was thrown out of the church for the belief that God wanted us all to prosper. Seeing as the book was written one-hundred-and-four years ago, I guess I could understand that. The interesting thing about Wallace Wattles is that he is who inspired Rhonda Byrne to write *The Secret*. That book is also transformational.

Wallace Wattles' little gem was just what I needed. He took the notion of don't give a man a fish, but teaching him how to fish was the answer. Wattles believed the more people on this earth who are successful the better. Not in today's world though, where the wealthy hold all the wealth. Making money and earning a good living was not a sin. This kind of flew in the face of the church of that time in history trying to convince us we are all sinners. I sure as hell am not. I am going to move off God and get down to business. I will leave it as this. I don't pray and ask for anything. I give thanks to God every day for all that I have.

I believe Wattles had it right. He was a great minister who was ahead of his time. His belief was that the world is full of abundance. There are more than enough resources for everyone. It all starts with believing that notion. Wattles understood people and the underpinning idea that we all want an abundant life for ourselves and our families. This book had a huge aha moment for me. In fact, there were several inspirational parts that made me stop and think. I needed to take this hand full of photocopies that I had all scratched up and actually buy the hard copy edition. It needed to have more value that a handful of paper held together I had put in a presentation folder. So here was this minister in the early 1900s talking about business. That's my kind of church! Wattles explains how a business transaction should take place. This is accomplished by helping others so they too will grow.

An aha moment was when he explained that as long as there is more value than your customer paid for the product the price is irrelevant. Yes, read that again. The price is irrelevant. Provide more value than the customer paid you for the product. This confirms the win-win philosophy beyond any doubt. I closed the book and reflected on that for a moment just to let it sink in. That statement changed everything for me on how I conducted business from that day on. We have all heard the sales experts explain to us how with our bag of tricks how we can move the customer to this point. I disagree with that as this tactic still focuses on the money. This way I take money off the table right at the beginning. *The Genie is out of the bottle.*

To make his point, Wattle uses as an example the way earlier settlers of North America trading guns for pelts with the natives. Guns that were perhaps worth $20 and one could trade them for furs that were at that time worth $50. The Native Americans were not duped out of $30 dollars. They now had a gun that would enable them to obtain more pelts faster than they could ever have done before. Both groups gained from the transaction and both became more prosperous. I began buying into this abundance notion in a big way. I live in a less populated area of Canada and for us to grow our business, we have to look outside our region to grow. To be successful if we stay at home, we need to have a huge market share. When I look out the window of the plane, just before I land in a major city, I smile and say to myself, "If I get just one percent of that market down there I will be hugely successful."

I trust you know your company's value proposition. Do you have it communicated in such a way that it is easy to grasp from the customer's viewpoint? If your company charges more than the competition, it is not a bad thing. You just have to be able to justify the value and understand that not every prospect will buy into that notion. Lexus and Toyota are made by the same company. We pay more for a Lexus because there are more features and luxury value. The customer who wants to be surrounded in the lap of luxury is prepared to pay the extra price for the Lexus. To the customer who sees a car a just a means of transportation would never consider purchasing a Lexus. They will buy the Corolla. Don't beat your head against the wall trying to sell the Corolla customer a Lexus.

There is no loyalty in price. The people who buy on price will drop you like a hot potato once the business up the street sells it for less than you do. Ask yourself, do you really want to get involved in this game? The crowd follows trends and fads. Trends and fads that are so price sensitive there is very little profit margin left. I can tell you the last race you want to win is the race to the bottom. Walking, talking and smelling the rest is not unique. If you want to sell a product for a reasonable profit I suggest you stay as far away from the crowd as possible. Less competition means more opportunity for profit. The price-conscious crowd thinks that business people who charge more are gougers. They have this perception that we know is unfounded. Trying to convince this price conscious group why you're worth more is an exercise in futility. Don't waste your time. Profit is not a dirty word.

When you're in the business-to-business world the business transaction is much different. It becomes a corporate spend versus a personal spend. There is more focus on value. In that world, there is more repeat business than shopping for a dress or a pair of pants. There are, however customers in that world who are purely focused on price – those who want a Lexus at the Corolla price, and in their mind they believe they deserve it. They have a huge purchasing volume and they demand every last cent. I avoid these customers whenever possible. I can sense them out at the beginning and I don't budge on price. They usually go away. A good thing! However, when we have a customer who insists on being treated like they are special we have a problem. I can tell you I have fired many customers over the years and telling them to take the long walk off a short wharf is often the best thing you can do for your business. It's bloody liberating. Wattles had it right. Only deal with those who understand and are willing to pay you for the value.

Stripped right down to it, we have to understand what our time is worth. Why spend all this time on a low margin customer? If you are top-line focused instead of bottom-line focused, you have it all wrong. The top line is for bragging rights. The bottom line reflects the value we place on our time. It's just like they say in golf. Drive for show and putt for dough. It takes a leap of faith to do this, however I can confirm the leap is worth it.

If you're having sleepless nights worrying about how you're going to deal with an unruly customer, it's time to push him off the dock. Not only will you have personal satisfaction but your staff will thank you too. They are likely wondering why are you putting up with this idiot? Focusing on where you will find profitable customers is a far better exercise in time well spent. If you want to really feel good, provide the 'get-lost customer' with the telephone number of your competitors.

"Here's the telephone number for ABC company. I'm certain they will be more suited to your needs." Come on! Tell me you're not smiling right now and thinking about what customer you're going to fire. Wattles would be proud of you for that and so would I.

What we all should come away from in this chapter is to have a full understanding of the connection between value and price. We have to be able to put our egos in the garage and stop chasing volume. Volume is important. It's far better to own a smaller, more profitable company than a bigger unprofitable one. Where there are skinny profit margins there is harder work to earn enough money to pay your staff and yes yourself too. In this case, 'more for less' is a fallacy. Get your head around that and you will be a less stressful person. If you're saying to yourself, "I just need to run a little harder," you're in trouble. If you start working on your business instead of in your business, you will find those profitable customers who understand your company's product and value.

If you are not the owner of a business and you are looking for a great place to land, I suggest you find a smaller company clear of the corporate world. You will be treated like a human and not a commodity. Small business owners have a true connection with their staff and their customers. These people work for their customers and not their shareholders. It's about much more than just extracting profit.

I must share an experience I had while trying to put together a deal with a big internet provider. The potential customer was demanding us to sharpen our pencil. He was pushing the fact that his customer had a large pension fund, and if we win this there would be potential for huge returns for both of us. I said, "Pardon me! A pension fund! No thank you." The squeeze from a customer like this would be never ending with razor thin margins.

I have worked for a family owned business and I have also worked for a large corporation. If you want a working life of being valued and not measured to death, I suggest you go find a great small business to work for. It's unlikely you will be downsized in the next recession and you will probably earn a better living while feeling a great sense of satisfaction in your role.

Success lies with under-promising and over-delivering. Customers always find great joy in getting more than they expected. The result is the same whether it's in the business-to-consumer or business-to-business environment. There is nothing worse than the sweetness of a great price followed by the sour taste of a lousy product. If you maintain the mindset of under-promise and over-deliver, you will be successful. If you provide more in value than you charge for your product or service you will successful beyond your wildest dreams. Thank you Wallace Wattles for taking price off the table.

Provide great value.

A product's value is much like success. It is different for everyone. It's easy to lose sight of this if you're wrapped up in the numbers. Listen to your heart. It's only a foot away from your brain. Your wallet or purse is three feet away.

CHAPTER TWENTY

I CAN MAKE A DIFFERENCE

Key Concept:
You never have to. You choose to.

I ask what are you doing for the good of others in your community or around that world for that matter? There is more to life that getting up every morning and doing your daily routine at work or running the kids to band practice and soccer. As an active volunteer I hear the constant cry, 'I just don't have the time.' I'm not sure just what the real reason is, however, I expect that we are spending so much time multi-tasking what we actually accomplish during the run of a day that it becomes cloudy. It's a competitive world out there and all volunteer driven organizations are scrambling for help and feet on the ground to deliver on their missions and outcomes. Social media is full of such causes constantly looking for your support. Many of us become involved in organizations as a result of someone we know suffering from a disease or a special needs group.

I had spent the last three years as Membership Chair for Rotary International in Atlantic Canada. It has been like a full-time job helping the forty-six clubs in our district grow their membership. We had a great team on our committee who wanted our organization to continue and flourish. The biggest challenge is to convince clubs that steeped in tradition to become relevant. The clubs that are relevant, exciting and fun grow. Those that don't make their meeting fun and enlightening continue to flounder. Our district has been one of the top performers in North America because we work at it. We value what our organization does. Just like in business, we had to become creative and make sure our message resonates with those who want to serve. My friend Paul, a Rotary leader in Quebec City, once did a presentation titled *"Close the Back Door."* The presentation was based on the theory if your Rotary Club was a business would you buy from it? Happy customers keep coming back.

It's easy to put off making a commitment to get involved because we worry how it will fulfil us, if we commit. Do you really have the time? There are so many choices. Where to get involved? You could join a church, the local hospital as well the barrage of health-related organizations like the Heart and Stroke Foundation or the Alzheimer's Society. If you don't choose to become involved, you won't have to worry about it. Is that an excuse to not get involved? What is the fear associated with becoming involved? I expect its commitment.

I became involved in Rotary because I wanted to get connected to the town I just moved to, both socially and for business reasons. More importantly, I wanted to give of my time for the better good of my community and the world. Not only do the organizations we get involved with grow, but we as individuals grow too. It's important that we get involved for emotional reasons. We have a connection to the cause. I find the organizations we want to tell the whole world about are the best ones to be connected with.

Rotary has become my community. Belonging to something that we feel connected to is good medicine for us all. I feel it helps us take our lives outside our work and our families. I call it 'the world view.' The reason Rotary works is that we all want to make the world a better place to live by enriching the lives of others. This organization does this in spades as those who want to be connected to the local projects can do so while other members are wanting to be involved in drilling wells or building schools in Africa. Although the members may have different interests, the common bond is with being alongside like minded people. It's very unique. I can walk into any of the world's 33,000 plus clubs and be welcome. It is the only organization in the world that has a seat at the United Nations that is not a country. World peace and understanding are cornerstones of the organization.

When I was at a low point in my life after my divorce, I stepped back from Rotary, as I felt I was unable to properly give and serve. I needed to focus on me. Once the word was out to my Rotary friends, they started to show up at my door to see how I was doing. This outpouring of deep care will remain with me all of my life. It was through Rotary that I met my second wife, Stella.

Rotary has a simple moral code for personal and business relationships. We call it the Four-way test:

1. Is it the truth?
2. Is it fair to all concerned?
3. Will it build goodwill and better friendships?
4. Will it be beneficial to all concerned?

Stripped right down to it you can see why the countries of the world who wanted to form the United Nations wanted Rotary to help with its creation. Rotary is in fact like my church – a church where we don't have a prayer. We just go out and do in the world in an effort to make it a better place to live. It's about a willingness of its members to feel good about helping others. It makes them feel good!

There may be times we have to forget the four-way test and do what's right. The world of compromise does not always draw the line down the middle of the page which would leave number two and four tests to some interpretation. The important thing is that all efforts are made to accomplish these four Rotary ideals.

The writing of this book and my involvement in a new business has needed much of my attention and pulling back from Rotary has always been tough for me. I have sipped the Kool Aid, which makes the pulling back even harder. Being half a Rotarian to me is much like many things we are involved in. Where do we find the time to be a volunteer? I just know that stepping back temporarily is much better than burning out.

I have friends outside of Rotary who sometimes look at me in amazement and bewilderment of what I do. I have always taken the approach I would rather be a small fish in a big pond than a big fish in a little pond. When you get involved in an organization that has a world view you might be surprised how big a fish you become in the big pond. Life is about growing our well being and not just our assets. The car that sits inside our garage really isn't a measuring stick of who we are. I suggest we look at this selfishly for a moment. Being a volunteer is good for the image of you and your company. You are seen as a caring individual. Don't you want that for you and your company?

The key is to give unconditionally. Do it with the expectation that you will get nothing in return other than it makes you feel good to give. I expect that your dog or cat loves you unconditionally. Feels pretty good, doesn't it? The reward is a rub behind the ear or a pat on their side. The wagging tail when you come through the front door at home can lift up your day. Giving unconditionally frees us from keeping score. Generosity doesn't always have to be in the form of a cheque.

When we give one gift to a group the returns often come back in multiple forms. As a Certified Coach I get asked to make presentations from time to time. I do it for free with no expectation of return. Often, my phone will ring or it arrives in my inbox. Can we get together? I need your services. It's important to be patient and not wait for the gift to come back. It always does when you least expect it!

If you're not already volunteering, thinking about becoming a volunteer I recommend you take your time in choosing the organization you wish to belong to. You want to choose what is important to you and your beliefs. It's also important to know what is expected of you and your time once you become involved. Be sure the organization you choose aligns with your passion. Volunteer organizations are usually committee driven and the process can be cumbersome for action minded business types, but the results will often outweigh the frustrations.

Finding an organization that has diversity in its cultures and services will broaden your horizons. Not only does Rotary have programs locally and internationally, but groups within the Rotary have similar interests. Rotary has fellowships like skiers, Harley Davidson owners, the fellowship of sailing Rotarians and so on. If you're involved in this organization, you have to have good morals and core values. If you don't have enough of a world view other than watching CNN, get involved.

Like most things in business, we need to schedule our volunteer time. There will always be a fire to put out at work. The only time I miss a weekly get together is when a blaze that can be extinguished with a garden hose grows to the firehose variety. I go early to socialize with my many friends and hear how they are doing and their news. Who says involvement has to be all work. I also look for advice from members who have a different skill set than us. We share openly. There is never an invoice that arrives in the mail.

I bring this back to making it a *choice to*. If it's a *have to*, you are involved with the wrong organization or being a volunteer is not cut out for you. Being a volunteer it not a prerequisite to being successful. There is no single recipe for success which we eluded to earlier, but it's a pretty big piece of the success pie in my world. The best advice I can give is that you look for the good things that will happen to you for giving of your time and your talents. I never look at this as charity. When we help others grow, we grow too.

You never have to. You choose to.

If you're struggling to find commitment, it's likely a 'have to.' Committing to what you chose to do is the frosting on the cake.

CHAPTER TWENTY-ONE

BROTHERLY LOVE

*Key Concept:
Focus on value, not price.*

It was while I was in the human resource business, I came across a sailing friend named Rod who asked if I was interested in selling for his marine business. I said I would be while I was trying to build my HR business. I spent close to a year in industrial marine sales and I wasn't able to grow the sales to the point where I could make a decent living. It was not worth the energy I was putting into it. It was extremely competitive and we did not have a strong listing of brand-name products to sell. The industrial marine supply business was also experiencing a consolidation much like I went through with the office products business. I knew I needed to move on, but to where was the question.

I spoke about meeting Bob at a networking event. He was a certified Neuro-Linguistic Programming (NLP) coach. As in the past, I was always looking for the edge that professional help could get me. I invested in a few sessions with Bob. That was an interesting exercise. Ironically, Bob also came to the same conclusion about the issue with my mother that I went through with Peter. This added a lot of clarity for me, as my wife had greater financial means, and I always felt my lifestyle was not really earned because she had deeper pockets than me. Bob helped me push past that by helping me realize that money is not the only measure of success. He helped me realize that I brought a lot to the table that enhanced life for both of us.

All this new learning about me and my relationship with money was starting to set in. The main reason I went to Bob was to help me figure out a way to get into yacht sales without being in competition with my brother John. For those of you who have never been through an NLP session, it is an experience that will take you to a mindset that will shock you. It totally got me to a comfort level on how I would approach my brother John and convince him I would be the best thing that would happen to his company. I convinced John to hire me as a sales guy and we would both profit from the relationship. I was now in the floating real estate business and ready to light up the sales board. My knowledge of the sailing game matched with my people and selling skills added to the secret sauce. The strong brand John had built over the last twenty-five years would make for a winning combination.

John and I had very different views on how the relationship should work, but we figured it out. I actually came on as a contractor and not an employee. That relationship changed after I got my feet wet and it was to our mutual advantage for me to become a commissioned employee for insurance and tax reasons. John struggled with the fact that if I am straight commission. I could come and go as I pleased with the exception of weekend days that I would be on office duty. I was cool with that. One thing for sure I knew that I needed to be on straight commission if I was going to be able to have some control over my time. Selling yachts is a demanding business that is a seven day a week job.

Well I had a blast, and I was selling boats like gangbusters. This was a long way from being the owner of a successful business but I was wearing deck shoes and khaki pants or shorts to work every day. I was still a partner in the marina at this time although not active on the marina property site. My years of yacht racing and at the marina provided me with a huge network of people to help with their yacht buying experience. John had wisely invested in a customer contact relationship software package called Maximizer. Maximizer was the precursor to the now popular Sales Force CRM which took the data collection of prospects to a new level. Maximizer had a sea of information that provided me with a bevy of ready prospects to call on. There was so much low hanging fruit the possibilities seemed endless.

My success came from being educational with the buyers on the characteristics of certain boat manufacturers strengths and weaknesses. John was a huge help to me in that area as well with his knowledge base. The hardest part about yachts sales is bringing the owners to a place where they are realistic about the value of their boat. Unlike real estate, yachts are a depreciating asset. Sailboats drop in value about five percent per year. Buying the boat is the easy part. It costs upwards of $10,000 per year to own a sizable sail or power boat. My strength was educating both the buyers and the sellers the real value and the expectations. The competition didn't only come from the other folks in the business, but the arm chair know-it-all sailors who would be coaching buyers in the background. I would lose a few deals every year to these pretend experts, but that's life and when you have enough deals on the go it just becomes mutable noise.

I estimate that seventy-five percent of the boat business is largely dependent on the internet to drive sales. This means that the lowest priced boat in its class and model becomes the starting point of price in the customer's mind. If you are going to be asking for more money you need to provide good evidence why your boat is worth more. Eastern Canada is a relatively small market for yacht sales, but when the Canadian Dollar went to being worth more than the US dollar in 2008, it changed our marketplace dramatically. Halifax is only 360 nautical miles from Boston, which is a huge boating market. People could buy a boat down there for twenty percent less, by the time they factored in the exchange. That meant I was now selling US boats and making fifty percent less money because the commissions were being split four ways. I was selling tons of boats and making less money. It was a dog's breakfast.

I had learned long ago about putting a value on my time and I was not going to work this hard for smaller commissions and the extra costs of doing business in the U.S. The paperwork alone to bring in a boat from the U.S. was crippling. It was time to get out. Many of the other brokers in the business asked me why are you getting out? You sell more boats than many of us. I was living in a world where the work life balance was way out of whack.

I had done well enough in the business that I built up a nest egg in my commission account. I took out enough money to live comfortably and left a nice stash in my commission account for a rainy day. A rainy day was an understatement. It was pissing rain. The shrinking percentage on the commissions was eating away at the reserve fund. I had always told John that the day my commission surplus is gone is the day I leave the yacht business. That day came in February 2009. I told John I was leaving. He and his accountant had worked out what they felt would be a good compromise for me to stay. We tried, that but the relationship changed as I was now taking a salary. I have never been one to be measured and John was a measurement type of guy. Proof there are different ways to be a success and John beyond a shadow of a doubt was successful. That being said, our arrangement lasted three weeks.

I have been successful in sales and building business based on many factors. I have always been client-focused and listened intently for their perceptions, real or otherwise. I always looked at things from the long term. I worked hard to take buyer's remorse off the table. That philosophy has stood me well over the years and I was always getting referrals based on my knowledge and professionalism. During my two years in the yachts sales business, I was paid a tip by two buyers for the exceptional service I provided. I took satisfaction in that and it confirmed beyond doubt that I was trustworthy and credible – two of the most powerful words I live my life by.

I could be accused of jumping ship and I should have perhaps stayed and rode out the storm. There was more to the decision to leave than money. That being said, as I look back on the industry today I made the right choice. The yachting world is a mature industry and there is an over-supply of boats on the market. Where there are bargains there is not much money to be made. The buyer is focused on price and as you will have learned from my previous chapters that I am not a price point seller. I used to be focused on price early in my business life and focused on my top line. Wisdom gained over the years has taught me to focus on what is left after the sale. There is nothing wrong with 'I'm worth more than that.' You just need to be able to back that up.

Education is key when we are dealing with buyers who want to make a substantial purchase like a yacht. It can be a features based process, however adding to the discussion the buyer's expectations is what cements the deal. We always joked about the two happiest days in a boat owner's life. The best is the day they bought the boat and the second best day is the day they sold the boat. It takes disposable income to be a boat owner. If you're in the how much are the payments group give that a second thought. The smaller power boat business has survived the storm based on payment plan buyers. Step back and think how you will feel when that $400 comes out of your bank account in February while the boat is under cover and two feet of snow in the back yard. This can also be said for the snowmobile crowd in July.

I take this back to the day when I was selling life insurance. I was not on the leaderboard, but I was at the top of the customer retention list. I could not sleep at night knowing pushed a buyer to purchase. The added weight of regret for both of us just isn't worth it. We don't get referrals when we sell like that.

Five years earlier, I went to purchase a car. I would usually purchase buybacks from a dealer. Cars that are one-year-old are my choice because the previous owner took the biggest bite out of the depreciation. I made the decision to buy, and I was happy. When I got home, I saw that the Michelin tires that were on the car got switched out for a new set of very cheap tires. I approached the dealer and they said that the tires were bad and they had gone to the dump. That car dealer who has over 1,000 employees will never get a sale from me again based on the tactics of one bad employee. It's that simple. A company is only as strong as the weakest link.

The internet has changed everything in the market place. It has created a price sensitive world based on the lowest possible price. We in North America have real value all screwed up in my view. If you're a business owner or a salesperson, the race to the lowest price is a race you don't want to win. If you're a realtor and you list a house for the price the seller wants you are doing both of you a disservice. The house will not sell and you will have wasted your time. I learned in the boat business that your first offer will often be your best offer. I coached many a buyer out of a low ball offer. If you want the boat, insulting the seller with a low ball offer is not a relationship building exercise.

I once sold a boat that the buyer was insistent on bargaining the price to the lowest point. When he took delivery of the boat, he asked me where is the ship's clock and other items. I told him the owner was prepared to leave those accessories on board, but after beating him up so much on the price, he took them off the boat. I rest my case on focusing on price. Wallace Wattles had it right.

You know when we always tell the truth, we don't have to remember what we said. When we focus on value, and not the price, is easier to come to peace with ourselves about the purchase. When we hold out for too much money when we are selling we need to be cognizant of the time value of money. If it takes a year to sell your boat and the carrying cost is $10,000 annually, it makes turning down an offer that was two or three thousand dollars seem ridiculous. When we focus on the value, we will always come out ahead. This philosophy will lead to a life of happy sailing.

Focus on value, not price.

The time to stop shopping is immediately following the purchase. If you bought it based on price disappointment is as close as poor quality or the next television commercial.

CHAPTER TWENTY-TWO

I TRUST YOU

Key Concept:
Routine is critical to accomplishment.

Whenever my best friend and first Cousin David comes to town from Ottawa we usually get together with a mutual sailing buddy Willy T. No, not the pirate ship anchored at the Bite in the British Virgin Islands. Willy T is his sailing name, but goes by Bill. The three of us have been sailing together since we were in our early twenties. We usually head down to one of the waterfront restaurants for a meal and a wobbly pop. Well, usually more than one. Willy T has no hair left. I'm bald on top and David still has a full head of hair, but its as white as the driven snow. We are anything but grumpy old men! Three Jack Lemmon is more like it.

We ended up at Stayner's Wharf, and I drew the short straw so I was the designated driver. One small glass of wine was it for me with my meal. We were not settled in very long when I told the boys that I had left the yacht business the previous day. I told them the story and they went quiet. "You're kidding, right?" they said. Nope. I'm not going to work that hard for such little money and pay my own expenses to boot. I'll be alright. They both knew that John and I differed on some things, but I wasn't going to go there. John's my brother. I love him and we are not going to talk about that. I have been out of work in the past, and I have always been able to land on my feet. Besides, I'm getting too old to be climbing up ladders and crawling under boat covers in the middle of the winter. It's a game for guys younger than me.

We chit chatted about the upcoming Marblehead to Halifax Race which we had done together for years. We were going on a forty-four-footer out of Toronto. David was going to do the delivery down to Boston with the owner and some of David's sons friends. I had been working hard to skirt around discussing my work situation and also that my decision also made things a little tough at home at the moment seeing I was not earning a living. Stella had been through this with me before when the HR business went south.

Willy and David had a couple of more glasses of Vino Tinto before we headed off for home. We dropped David off at his hotel and then I went on to drop off Bill. When we got to Bill's house he said to me just before he got out of the car. "Why don't you swing by the office on Friday and we'll have a chat." Bill has always been one to hold his cards close to his chest, so I didn't probe. The twenty-five-minute drive home to Bedford left me having more questions than answers.

Friday arrived, and I swung by Bill's office. Bill had owned the business for almost twenty-five years. As I was waiting in the lobby, I remembered when he bought the business and it was a room full of telephone operators working on old cord boards where they connected calls and took messages. It was all done by hand back then. I walked in to see Bill, and he said, "I'd like it if you would come to work for us. I don't like salespeople, and I have not had good luck whenever I hired them. All I know is that you would do a great job and I trust you."

He slid an offer across the desk and I reviewed it. It wasn't a lot of money, but the commissions had a good upside. Come the third year, I would be making good money when the renewals started to kick in.

It took me a good year to get the hang of the business. Understanding the scripting and capabilities of the software was a big undertaking for me. I was struggling with the type of customers we had as it was mostly after-hours business working for plumbers, electricians and oil companies. It was like selling widgets and not very exciting. I was looking for something more exciting and strategic than trying to get contractors to pay what the service was worth. I discussed the possibilities with Bill of going after more daytime business doing customer service work and becoming an extension of our customer's business. He agreed we should test the waters.

Gradually, the business started to roll in as we had more and more daytime customers. We were winning some pretty big contracts and it wasn't long before we had just as many staff members working the day time shifts as the evening shifts. Working for Bill was a real treat. He didn't micro-manage and let people do their own thing.

One time, early on, I told Bill that I wasn't pleased with my results. He simply replied, "There is no need for me to put any pressure on you, you put enough pressure on yourself to perform."

Who wouldn't want to work for a man like that? I wasn't the captain of the ship, however, being left on my own and how I grew sales was damn nice.

Four years into my role, I felt we needed to become a national player in the call centre business. The Toronto, Calgary and Vancouver markets was where all the action is, though I love Nova Scotia. The people are great, but the average person just doesn't see the big picture. What seems a lot of money at home is chump change in a bigger market. The low cost of telecommunications made it very easy for us to consider entering these markets. Bill, myself and Ian, our IT man, threw around some ideas on what our marketing plan should be. We interviewed three companies to do the website build and also for a company to enter us in the world of social media. It was a big spend. We did our homework and felt it worth the risk. Today, three-quarters of our new business comes from a distant market. It has allowed us to grow and at a nice and profitable pace.

Some seven years later, I am still here. A seasoned entrepreneur like me should be out doing his own thing. I got out of the marina business six years ago, but I managed to keep my fingers in the entrepreneurial pie by obtaining my Professional Coaching Designation. My secondary 'job' is in helping small business owners with advice on how to grow their business as well as working with companies in need of a turn around. I don't have a big customer list but it keeps me active in helping others avoid some of the problems I have been through in my business career. I was ever so cognizant not to be doing this on company time. I suspect these activities keep me in the business game.

Another reason I stay is that I am able to make an impact on where the company is headed and to do what entrepreneurs like to do. Grow business! I learned a long time ago I was great at building businesses but not so good in running them. This position allowed me the latitude to be making a difference. When I leave the office at the end of the day I'm not taking home the worries I did when I was self-employed. I have weeks where I work sixty hours and others thirty-five. Now in my sixties, I find I can't run sixty to seventy-hour weeks all the time like I used to.

The ultimate decisions are not mine and it took some time to get used to that. I do though have a say and I am heard. I don't get ruffled very easily, but when I do, I usually let everyone know my discomfort. While attending the National Convention CAMX for the telephone answering and call centre business in Las Vegas we heard Cameron Herold the author of the best-selling book *Double Double* make a presentation. Cameron is an expert on cutting to the chase and finding deficiencies. One tip Bill instituted was the 'ten-minute management huddle' three days a week. It has made a huge difference on how we operate and communicate. All of our roles are interdependent, and it can be frustrating to have a new customer roll out being stalled by one of the other departments in the business. During the ten-minute huddle, each of us says what we have on our plate and the issues they are having. I can tell you the system works.

When I know what they have on their plate I can be more understanding why things are held up. They also get to know what my challenges are in winning deals. Solutions to these issues often float to the surface.

I fight back the notions that I wimped out and I have not started another business. I am in a pretty good financial position at this stage of my life and throwing some money at a new business is a risk that I'm not sure I want to take. I am finding other ways to have an impact on my life and the lives of others. Projects like writing this book have been very fulfilling. I can tell you I have approached this book like it is a business, and I am grateful I hired good advice to make sure it would be impactful and successful at the same time. Every word written is mine, but understanding the content and how to present content is an area I don't know well. I am working for someone else's company, but I am making a difference from my expertise gained from all my years as an owner. Every business needs wisdom and a sobering second thought before charging down a road that you don't know where it is going to end.

I learned from all the years I spent in mature industries that we have to be able to adapt to change. Change is going to come at you surer than heck. Change is your friend and not your enemy. The sooner you come to that understanding, the happier and more successful you will become. The telephone-answering business was a mature business that came under threat by the telephone companies when answering machines and voicemail took over. Consumers and businesses flocked to get one of those machines. It would save thousands. I ask how personal is an automated phone attendant that says, "We value your business. Please listen to the following options so we can serve you better." We grew the business in spite of this threat from technology by catering to the business who knew the value of having a human answer their phone. Did you know that eighty percent of first time callers to your business hang up when they are greeted by an auto-attendant?

I suggest you find a way to make the work you do meaningful for you and your employees. When we know we are appreciated by both our employers and our customers, we want to come to work. The pay scale is number three on the list of why people work where they do. Being appreciated and having an impact is number one and two. Many readers already know this, but we are all guilty of not thanking our employees enough and recognizing them for what they do. These people are the lifeblood of your business.

Very few of us like routine, although it can be critical to the success of getting this accomplished. Employees want freshness in their work. There is nothing like a project to find improvements and defficiencies that get their juices flowing. Projects that are collaborative and create team spirit bonds our employees and they all rise to the challenge and the sense of accomplishment when on launch day of a new product. Wrestling with the bear to find a new business process that they will all be proud of is huge for morale. They're worth it! Go challenge them. They will love you for it.

Routine is critical to accomplishment.

Practice doesn't make you perfect, it makes you better. The routine of getting the things you don't like to do behind you first allows you to always finish on a high note.

CHAPTER TWENTY-THREE

SEVEN GUESTS

Key Concept:
Take time to say and do it right.

I have met many wonderful people in my life, I can't help but feel blessed. I have had so much disappointment and bad luck over the years that I have come to the conclusion that most of us on the planet have had adversity in our lives. It is how we react to those challenges that define who we are. I have a business and friends network that is in the thousands so I have come across many who have rebounded from a downturn in their lives. My own setbacks have given me a keen sense to be on the lookout for people who have overcome adversity and how they live their lives today. Let's forget for the moment all those people who post positive sayings on Facebook. I'm talking about those who get up and do it every day. The world needs cheerleaders. It needs a hell of a lot more resilient people.

I managed to survive a bankruptcy, two businesses with financial losses and three job losses over a fifteen-year period. I have every reason to feel like a victim. I refuse to do that. What I have learned both as a business person and a human being is to never give up. I want to live a long, happy and prosperous life. That can't be accomplished by doing the same old same old. Happiness is a choice.

It may seem strange, but I have come to a place of gratitude in my life for all that I have. What I have now often came to me wearing scars. I have been blessed to have had the opportunities that came to me. I feel blessed to have had the guts to get back up and keep going. The old saying good luck is about putting yourself in a position to be lucky is true. Most importantly, I had people who believed in me that helped me through the rough patches in my life. Much of the success in my life has come as a result of my people skills. I have learned a way to get people to tell me their inner thoughts. That's because I make it about them. Life and relationships are tightly bound to our emotional being. Women are so much better at this than men, because they are more willing to show their vulnerabilities. As for men! What do you really have beneath those peacock feathers anyway?

I wanted to do something unique for some people I had noticed as doing amazing things in their lives. These people suffered near life ending experiences, physical and mental challenges and while putting others before themselves. I decided to have them over to my house for dinner and to tell them why I think they are so special. I wrote them all individually and told them my plan and why they inspired me. Would you come to meet some other great people like yourself? They all said yes. Phew. I wasn't so sure this plan I hatched would work out. One person Frances was unable to make it due to business travel commitments.

To introduce everyone I wrote the following letter to them all:

"By way of introduction, I will provide a brief reason why I feel so inspired by you all. This is really about you. I /we will want to share more on the eighth. You are a group who shows great humility so saying something after I expand a bit about you is optional.

I introduce.

Annie: Annie was born with a neurological disorder that kept her speechless for several years early in her life. Annie required one on one special education schooling until she entered junior high school. Annie progressed and managed to graduate with the standard academic class from high school by way of her own determination. She had applied to go to university but because of her schooling history was granted one semester on a trial to see how she managed. The story gets better. She passed the first semester with honors.

Mike: While in a high speed chase during his career in the RCMP he flipped his cruiser resulting in a broken back that left him paralyzed and unable to walk for close to two years. Through strenuous physio and brute determination, he was able to walk again under his own steam. He is a devoted volunteer to youth and has a successful career in conflict resolution, that magnify his people skills.

Vivienne: I first met Vivienne four years ago when she moved to Halifax and she joined our Rotary Club. Vivienne arrived from Ontario having come out of an unhappy relationship with her husband and business partner. Her son was going to university in Halifax and she came to support him. Vivienne came looking for a fresh start and I watched her grow from what appeared to be this very unhappy person to the person she is today. She is truly inspiring. Vivienne will flower wherever she is planted.

Luke: I also met Luke through Rotary. The more I got to know Luke, the more I realised his passion for lasting change and especially for youth. Luke is involved in so many projects it's hard to imagine where he finds the time. Luke's business a sport shoe, ski shop and a clothing company that was chosen by Nike Corporation as the top store in the world (independent stores) for Community and Humanitarian work in 2012 for Nike dealers.

Lorna: I met Lorna ten years ago through friends of my wife Stella. Lorna was the happiest person I had ever met. She sees joy in everything and has the great ability to laugh at herself first. Lorna has survived two rounds of life-threatening cancer treatments including a bone marrow transplant. Positive attitude wins the day every time.

Peter: I first met Peter four years ago at a networking event. Right away I knew this guy was different. Peter has embraced becoming a father in his late forties and lives his life with total passion in spite of living with Parkinson's disease. Peter learned first-hand that he could not hold back denial of his condition to now helping others suffering from limited abilities and beliefs to learn to live life on your own terms.

I look forward to having you all meet each other on the eighth. Please feel free to ask any questions you may have. Please remember to bring your spouses so they can share in this joyous occasion.

The seventh person, Francis, was unable to come. She inspired me because she was uprooted from her teaching career in Texas to move to Halifax so her husband could finish his postgraduate work. Frances dove into the community and tried her hand at network marketing. She eventually ended up starting one of the first social media companies of the era. She has grown her business to now be international and recognized for being the second fastest growing company in Atlantic Canada. Her success comes from her ability to over deliver on expectations.

I struggled with how this would go as I wanted this to be about them. Who was I to think they were special? They truly inspired me and I just felt they needed to know and this gathering came from someone who had nothing to gain from holding this event. Yes, this made me feel good. It was my way, I suppose, of insuring what they accomplished in their lives wasn't going unnoticed. Yes, some of the attendees have been recognized in a more official manner from organizations, but this was at the most basic level. This came from a level of friendship and genuine respect. I held to the thought that someone like myself with little significance managed to notice what they had accomplished.

I thought that after everyone had arrived, I would get to the brief ceremony of introducing them and telling the group why I thought they were special and why they inspired me. All but one spoke following to expand one their story and also to thank me. Each was so humble, and this alone added to the group I had invited. I had presented each of them with framed plaques that stated their name and they were counted as friends who inspired me. There were some tears and some laughter, but it all went better than I could have imagined. The comfort level in the room was now a relaxed state. Some of the guests knew each other and some had common interests. I had managed to have the dining room table set so all could sit at the same table and the feast of great food and wine began.

One of my wishes was they would get to know each other better and talk about their stores with each other. I didn't speak much for the rest of the evening. They had taken over the conversations. Some conversations were quiet across the table and some for all to hear. It was joyous. Good food and wine at a table is the best form of gathering there can be. Even Stella, who had questioned my motives, was enjoying the evening. I had the best thank you from one of the attendees the next morning who wrote to say thanks for a wonderful evening and closed her letter by saying the world needs more Paul Roy's. Thank you Lorna!

One of the things I have learned from my ups and downs in life is to ask for help when I needed it. I truly believe that asking for help is a sign of strength and not weakness. The same can be said within our friendships or in our workplace. There is a big difference in asking for guidance so you may do the task properly than struggling through it on your own and getting it wrong. We shouldn't mistake this as them doing it for us, but helping us learn and get it right. Stripped right down, it's don't give a person the fish but teach a person to fish. We should not feel vulnerable when we ask for help. It is those folks who are vulnerable that effect real change. Looking at this in a different way, those who help others are often the ones who have others show up on their doorstep when they need a lift up. Where there is heartfelt emotion and understanding real things of goodness take place.

I became very aware that when I die, I don't want anything left unsaid. Each day that passes means you have one day less to do that. I ask how many times have you heard 'I didn't get to settle things with my sister or parent before they died?' My parents were there for me through thick and thin and I was determined they would know my gratitude before they died. I wanted nothing left unsaid. I have great peace knowing I did that and I have a clear conscience. I started an exercise a few years ago by writing letters of thanks to the people who have helped me in the past. It is a practice I recommend for anyone who is in gratitude for an act of caring and kindness. Saying it out loud doesn't cut it. Putting it in an email isn't much better. By taking the time to handwrite a letter of thanks adds to the importance of the words 'thank you.' It then becomes a deliberate act and not a reflex. Like the people who inspire me; I get the most amazing gratitude in return. It makes us both feel good.

The acts of deliberate gratitude are what separates us from the crowd. It builds bridges in our relationships. I keep a gratitude journal that I write in most every day. It is an opportunity for me to reflect on the greatness in life and people. By taking the time to write it down it has more meaning. It has a bigger impact. This multi-tasking world we live in distracts us from what is really important in life.

All the good stuff in life happens in our hearts and how we deal with our friends and co-workers. Taking the time to do and say it right will make a huge difference in your lives and the lives of all those you touch. Being unique isn't having a tattoo that no one else has. Being unique on a personal level speaks to the fact that you don't run with the herd. We all want to be a somebody! Being authentic is a great place to start.

Take time to say and do it right.

Actions do speak louder than words. Recognizing the greatness in others grounds us to what really matters. The sweetness comes when the right words are delivered at the right time and place.

CHAPTER TWENTY-FOUR

MEASURING UP

Key Concept:
Have a mentor.

When I was younger, it often felt like I didn't measure up to dad's measuring stick. He pushed me hard to perform at school, music and sports. If I heard it once I heard it a thousand times, "If you're going to do it, do it right!" You will recall from the first chapter he took hockey away from me for not being a top performer in the class. I resented that for years. I resented all the visits to the psychiatrist while in my teens as he wanted to get a bead on why I was such a hellion yet bright and talented. At the same time, he was taking me away for weekends on the boat and away fishing so I could learn to enjoy the great outdoors. Truth be known, he figured if I was with him there was less chance of me getting into trouble.

When dad died in 2015, we knew a couple of weeks beforehand that he was not going to pull out of this one. He was a heart specialist and deep down he knew too. He as always refused to give up. He left me with that trait too. My siblings decided that I would be the one to deliver dad's eulogy. I had spent the most time with him and knew him the best. This gave me a good while to put together a send off for the service that the whole family and all of his friends would remember for years to come.

I cried more that week and a half as I put together the eulogy than I had cried most of my life. I worked hard so that it was inclusive of all my family, but touched on his bigger-than-life personality that people at the service could relate to. There had been a snowstorm during the night of the gathering at the funeral home, but it didn't stop anyone. The church was full, as they were still clearing off the streets of Halifax and the church steps. The service went off without a hitch. Lots of laughter and tears. Numerous people came to me after the service and said, "Paul that was the best Eulogy I've ever heard." I wanted the eulogy to reflect the person he was. It was a great feeling of satisfaction knowing I really did know my dad.

I always knew when it was time for dad to go he would leave this planet kicking and screaming because he didn't want to go. I remember dad always mused about having a fancy car. I think he would have been about 85 or 86 when the old Ford wagon was ready to give in and he exclaimed to me that he was going to buy a nice Volvo. I said dad, "Volvos last a long time." Without missing a beat he asked me. "What's your point?" He never did buy the Volvo. There was always a new gadget or sail the boat needed. The boat or the cottage always won the day on where the disposable income landed. Over the last forty years, dad and I had created quite a friendship as we shared with each other our deepest thoughts, cares and concerns. Dad was totally unique. There was no one on this earth quite like dad. I loved him for that.

When dad graduated from high school he went off to university to be a forester. He loved the out of doors and being with his buddies in the wilderness. The bubble wrap parents of today would be a gash of the life he lived as a kid heading off into the wilderness for days with his shotgun and fishing rod. Back in those days, doctors were hard to come by. Dad's father was a family doctor, and his older brothers Wally and Lex were studying medicine. He was drafted into medical school and his life of medicine began.

Dad became a great doctor. Dad would have been good at anything he did, reflecting back on if you're going to do it you may as well do it well. He lived by that motto in everything he did in life. He was a magnificent teacher on how to live life. Dad was a doctor because he loved medicine. He wanted to help people remove their pain. He chose to be a pediatrician because children's pain was real and not caused by an abusive lifestyle. Dad was also a teaching doctor who was on faculty at Dalhousie Department of Medicine. When word got out in the medical community in Halifax, many of the doctors who studied under him would come by his hospital room to say hello and say how much they enjoyed his heart lessons during medical school. I was present with dad during many of these visits. Many of these doctors I also knew personally from the sailing and skiing communities. It was very heartfelt.

What separated dad from many of those in the medical field was his people skills. He was a people person first. He always asked who they were and where they were from. I suppose it came from the old Cape Breton tradition to ask "Who's your father?" He was better at this than Dale Carnegie himself and he never read the book. His patients and parents of his patients adored him. He knew how to get to the emotional part and work on putting them at ease. Outside of the medical field, be it in the yachting community or the sport fishing community people gravitated to dad. He always had a way to ask the right question. He could ask, "Now, what brings you here; better than anyone I know." If he didn't believe the answer he would ask, "Are you sure? It doesn't sound so?" They would reflect and give him the real reason. He was a master.

I understand from many of his now adult patients and parents of children with bad hearts still living, he was great at putting everyone at ease. As one could imagine with parents bringing in their sick infants the parents would spout off what the symptoms are with their child. Dad had a way of saying, "I'm the doctor here." Dad would get the children to tell them how they felt and where the pain was or was not. It worked because it was a conversation.

I grew up in the days before Medicare and social programs to support those in need of medical attention. This was back in the days when you paid the medical bills out of your own pocket. Often patients didn't have the money to pay. I remember the days of patients and parents of patients coming by the house at Christmas time with fresh fish, vegetables, lobster and many other things to offer their gratitude. It was a great lesson for me then a young lad about life and gratitude in its simplest form. Looking back, it helped shape the person I am today. We waited many a Christmas dinner for dad to come home from the hospital, having had to make an urgent assessment of a newborn with heart problems. He never grumbled as he went out the door, when it could have been so easy to stay.

Dad lost a lot of money backing me in my first business venture and I always felt a sense of obligation to help him at the house, on his boat or cottage as a form of repayment for all he did for me. Elizabeth was very understanding of this when the kids were younger. She too was a devoted family person. It was during those many weekends together that I really got to know my father. We would come in at lunch time after our chores, make a sandwich, have a glass of white wine, sit by the fire and recharge our batteries. My father always externalized his dreams while in front of the fire. Later in life, I took dad on annual spring road trips and went down just about every road we traveled in Eastern Quebec, Maine, New Brunswick and Nova Scotia. It became a ritual and he shared much of what he learned in life and I always enjoyed his stories some for the third or fourth time.

I swear the first books that dad read in his life were Tom Sawyer and Huckleberry Finn. Dad was a master at getting you to work on his projects. Not one bit of moss grew under my father's feet. It didn't matter if it was at the boat, the cottage or the house. Once the small talk was dispensed with it was, "Could you help me with this for a minute." My first hernia came trying to wrestle the float ramp up onto the dock after 'Do you have a minute?'

Canada's only had one go at trying to win the America's cup. My dad was involved. He was chair of a group of individuals who fund raised and built the yacht. When there became two competing groups dad once again became part of the merger of the two efforts. The Royal Nova Scotia Yacht Squadron was the club of record and Dad was the Commodore. He and mother moved to Perth, Australia to participate in the activities. To say that dad was a possibilities thinker would be an understatement. As I write this, one of his favorite sayings come to mind. "Why are you talking about it? Just do it!" I swear Nike took that line from my father.

Dad started an internet business when he was sixty-five. He wrote and published two books. The first book when he was eighty-eight and the second was in print run the week he died just before his ninety-second birthday. He pioneered heart operation procedures. He cut a record in his teens with a big band group in the late 1930s. He was destined to be a musician. As much as he loved music he knew a life in the music world would lead to a life of up and downs. Ebbs and flows.

Among all of his accomplishments, Dad was first and foremost a people person. Dad was a master at relationships. He knew how to bring out the best in others and was also great at talking about the sticky gooey stuff. The emotional stuff! I guess you could say Dad was a successful coach long before the business was invented. If it hadn't been done yet, dad was going to try it. He was a fierce competitor proving that nice guys can finish first.

You will recall back in the first chapter I said that I won the parent lottery. No, not the financial lottery! The life lottery. I have had many mentors in my life. People I emulated. People I wanted to learn from. My biggest mentor regarding life issues was my dad. He hated conflict and would cut to the chase to get things resolved. He also hung me out to dry a couple of times that became huge life lessons. I was extremely pissed off at the time, but when I look back at them, he really was saying, "It's your problem. You go fix it."

From my dad, I learned about love, humility, caring, drive, ambition, competition, being unique, to always do my best and most importantly, to live my dreams. He had all that wrapped up into one.

Not all of us are lucky enough to be born of parents with these skill sets like I was. This doesn't mean we can't learn them from others. Wisdom can be found in many places. I warn you to be cautious of those who advertise they are mentors. What it takes to be a good mentor is earned. We talked earlier about trust. It too is earned. I suggest you gravitate to those who are quietly successful. They are the ones who too learned from others. I can't express enough that you evaluate who you want to be first. Once you know what and who you want to become you put up your antenna and start looking.

You are already halfway there. You now know who you want to be. Now you can start to act like the person you want to be. You will gain laser focus on those who oppose what you want to become. Don't be afraid to ask them for their time. Tell them you admire them and what they have accomplished. I am interested in your field of expertise and how you do things. Can I have a half hour of your time? If they are truly the kind of person you want to be they will say yes. Think about that for a minute. Would you blow off someone who asked you for your opinion because they admire you? Exactly. Life is all about how you make the ask. This is not a time to let the fear of rejection stop you. If you can't get past that step you will struggle with much of what you want to accomplish in life. It took eleven years for me to meet an important mentor in my life. That was Jack Canfield. I studied his book for several years. I attended many of his free weekly seminars by conference call. To have him sign my old tattered copy of his book was a moment I will cherish the rest of my life.

My father began to pay me compliments by referring people to me who came to him for help or advice usually on personal issues. He would just say, "You will want to talk with my son Paul about that." I guess I was no longer being judged or measured. I had perhaps become the person he felt I should be.

Life is full of mentors. A mentor may not have the whole package you want, but they may have attributes you want to have. Study them and pattern yourself like them. If we are going to become our authentic self, learning from multiple mentors is a wonderful way to become the person you want to be. You're worth it after all, aren't you?

Have a mentor.

Mentors are all around us. It's through observation that they become very recognizable. It's part of the constant search for self-improvement. When asked, true mentors will take the time to help you grow. That is after all how they got there.

CHAPTER TWENTY-FIVE

A PEEK OVER THE HORIZON

Key Concept:
Live with gratitude, consistently.

I have traveled a lot of dusty roads in my day, and I still look forward to the journey. Occasionally I am asked about my business career. Following my brief summary others often seem perplexed. They wonder how I kept pressing on. It was simple. It all boiled down to a burning desire to make a difference and create a life filled with wins, big and small. Not all of them about money. I always knew if I surrendered I would wilt away and likely die early from boredom and regretting all the adventures yet not lived. I had a fuller life in my first fifty years than most would live in a lifetime. I'm at the time of writing this book sixty-two, and looking forward to many more adventures. No matter where in the world I have traveled, I have met the most amazing people and I say to myself, I could never pack in all I want to explore. Remaining to work helps fund that and it means I get up every morning with a purpose.

Each hit I've taken personally and in business moulded me to who I am today. I feel fortunate to live in a world where more understanding is gained as one of those who tried and failed from time to time. I prefer to say I came up short every now and then. Companies and people don't grow and prosper if they don't take chances and stretch themselves. Why should we feel bad when someone who settled for the ordinary makes a judgement about our failures and hiccups. I actually feel sorry for them not having lived life to its fullest. The lessons I learned from my failures are what molded me. We can be humble and hold our head high at the same time. I have lived this and I can confirm it actually builds credibility and respect. I have gotten up off my knees, dusted myself off numerous times. I have soldiered on. It was simple. I felt I was worth it.

I have always held myself accountable. When you hold yourself accountable you are in control, regardless of whether you are an employee or self-employed. When you're accountable it makes it tougher for others to control you. After all, you would only agree to be accountable to what you feel is acceptable. Do you see how easy it is to have some element of control? It's pretty simple once you agree to the terms. I ended up in the hospital during the final days of the office products business because of anxiety. My heart was racing uncontrollably. Why? Because, I lost control.

The folks who are behind the desks at the widget factory or the halls of government have very little control in their workplace. They may feel they are secure in their job, however it comes at a hefty price. Doing a job you don't like for thirty-five years to secure a pension is akin to being in jail as far as I am concerned. Being self-employed or a senior position in business is the only way to have control of you and your time, not the other way around.

I have tossed the word wisdom around much in this book and it is a wonderful place from which to make business and personal decisions. Wisdom comes from experience. It comes from both successes and failures. All the famous inventors like Bell, Edison and Franklin made numerous failed attempts before their idea became a reality. Why should life in our day and age be any different? When you have had some trip and stumble like me it's the fuel needed to make it right. That burning desire to succeed! I can't express enough that you ignore the judgements from those who have never tried.

They know not the joy to have succeeded. Wisdom is a place and a right of passage for those who wear the badge of courage. For they have tried, failed and then succeeded. The *woulda coulda shoulda* is for those faint of heart and those who have never stepped off the curb to play in traffic.

No one likes a 'been there, done that' or 'I told you so' type of person. We have all heard them. We smile and remain courteous. There is nothing to be gained by acknowledging or engaging in a discussion with these types of people. There is truth in the saying never get into an argument with a fool. You will lose because they will always be a fool. Controlling or turning off the background noise allows you to focus on what you need to accomplish. As long as you believe in your mind what is attainable is attainable you will be successful. That bright light at the end of the tunnel is not always a freight train.

They key is to enjoy what you do. Keep it fresh. People like projects for a reason. The end is near. The sense of accomplishment is so close you can touch it. If you're in the widget business projects are tough to come by. I was reminded by a close friend who is the son of a multi-millionaire on how opportunities came to his father. He had a steady stream of young business people looking for investors parading into his office, flogging an idea for their businesses or to launch a new idea. He might invest in one in ten opportunities because he liked the idea and it would make money. It wasn't charity. These opportunities kept his father young and brought a great feeling of helping hatch a new business. When you're successful, opportunities come to you. Many successful business people thrive on partnerships. Each brings a talent and they spread the risk. Freshness is the fuel to grow. Freshness is a very important ingredient of enthusiasm.

I have always attacked what I do with gusto. I have lived with the enthusiasm of a young man, gaining the wisdom of an older man through experience. I believe when you're building and growing a business the enthusiasm you hold is visible to those you are trying to sell your product or service too. They are likely thinking it has to be a good product for him or her to be so passionate about it. Learning to take your idea to market is where much of the talent is required. Many a great idea died from not being taken to market properly.

If you allow life to beat you up, you are in trouble. That may seem an obvious statement, but if you're too risk adverse you have become the ordinary. If you're happy in that space, that's great...though a stress-free life also comes at a price. A life without purpose ends much sooner than those who had the guts to step off the curb. I feel I have learned to master the setbacks. They're usually much smaller than you might think. When you expect them to always be there they aren't really set backs are they? They are obstacles. The obstacles are the validation tests to our goals and desires. You don't have it quite right yet.

I am convinced beyond a doubt that you need an exit strategy to be successful. A competitive race has a finish line. A masterful symphony has an end. A hockey game has a final buzzer. The key is to win. It makes no difference if you're a stockbroker or a company manager. What you have completed has to be meaningful. That's the journey part. When you plan for the end you will have built something worth having built. If you're a business owner, failure to have an exit strategy takes the need to grow and prepare your business for sale at a later time off the table. The key is to be able to finish on your terms.

For those of you that have read Jack Canfield you will know of the vision board. Writing goals down is key. Adding in images and pictures of those goals on the vision board increases your success rate. What's your vision for the future? If you don't have one, you better get one. Living on the ocean's edge was in my vision book thirty years ago. I have been living on the ocean now for fourteen years. That just didn't happen by chance. The blotter on my desk is clear. It has images under it of things I want to achieve in clear view right next to my keyboard.

Having an exit strategy will force you to integrate long-term decisions into your planning processes. It's all part of delayed gratification. Yes, you can take rewards along the way. Having your cake and eating it too is a wonderful thing. You want to grow your business into something someone else wants. That means you have retained earnings. Your business grows steadily. You have no or very little deferred maintenance. You have a solid staff and workforce. That is the foundation of a successful business. When you have what someone else wants you have full control of how your exit unfolds. If you take any of the previously mentioned cornerstones away what you have is worth much less.

Many businesses are bought and sold through some form of the seller taking back a mortgage or payment scheme as part of the transaction. Both of these methods allow you to be part of the business as you wind down. You're working in the business by choice. Without solid planning you will be working in the business to keep it alive and you need the income to simply exist.

Having an exit strategy allows you to translate your personal statement to your business. It's not all about the money. Having a healthy lifestyle and the balance sheet is critical. The key word in the previous sentence is balance. Legacy is also a powerful motivator. Seeing your business live on is a testament to you. It's only natural that what you built or help build lives on. There is a great satisfaction to that. If you have done it right, there will be money left at the end. The last time I checked river cruises in Europe costs money. Perhaps you might want to put to picture of that on your vision board. The point being, plan for the day you say *goodbye*.

Your exit strategy no matter your vocation allows you to live your life consistently. Each part of your journey is enjoyable, partly because of the prize that comes when you walk out the door. Your life's purpose lives in the journey. I can't emphasize enough - you will find your purpose, if you don't have one. Not only will you be happier so will your loved ones. Many champions of business and Olympians thrive on the goal. They also know that success comes from the routine of practice and workouts so they are ready for the big day. In business, there are lots of people willing to assist you with the routine because they don't like to stretch themselves. That plays into your hand of working on your business and not in your business. This doesn't make you a control freak. In fact, it's the opposite if you empower those who work for you.

Imagine your life filled with joy. Imagine living your life excited about your feet hitting the floor every morning. I believe having a strong sense of gratitude will help in living your life consistently. Make sure you go to bed happy. It will be the source of many a good night's sleep. Living aboard a rudderless ship can be a life filled with rough seas. When you keep your eyes on the horizon the rough waters between you there don't seem so rough after all. It's taking the trip toward the horizon that allows you to peek over the edge where a new adventure awaits.

Happy Sailing.

Live with gratitude, consistently.

The peace found in gratitude allows us to live in the moment. Appreciating what we have, helps us to live the dream of becoming who we want to be.

PAUL'S PRINCIPLES

1. Longevity = Love + Purpose
2. Our interactions are as unique as we are as individuals.
3. Sometimes, you just have to sit on the deck of the boat with a wobbly pop.
4. Progress = Perception + Mental toughness
5. Ask and you shall receive.
6. Beware of shiny things!
7. Do you want to be right or happy?
8. We need the lows to see the possibilities.
9. Let honesty and integrity lead.
10. Find out who is really the boss.
11. Have a unique value proposition.
12. Know when it's time to reinvent yourself.
13. The reward is unconditional giving.
14. Resilience will always trump survival.
15. The dots will connect. Be patient.
16. Make ideas float.
17. Your aha moment is coming!
18. Strive to continuously improve.
19. Provide great value.
20. You never have to. You choose to.
21. Focus on value, not price.
22. Routine is critical to accomplishment.
23. Take time to say and do it right.
24. Have a mentor.
25. Live with gratitude, consistently.

ABOUT THE AUTHOR

Paul has been writing articles on success and positive attitude now for five years preparing for the day he would write his first book *It Happened On Purpose*. Whenever Paul told his story listeners would always say you need to write a book. No one will believe it!

Paul's ADD fuelled a rush in and ask questions later attitude that took years to understand and harness. Two business failures, a firing from a public executive position and two marriages later, Paul still carries an optimism about life that is infectious.

Paul's people skills and desire to succeed helped him grow business as a result of his entrepreneurial spirit. He is also a serial volunteer who embraces giving his time and money as a way to focus less on self and more on lifting others. He believes his many setbacks in life amplifies having empathy for those in struggle. We are stronger as a result of our setbacks.

This book is an extraordinary story of resilience and passion for life. We all love story tellers and this book contains so many nuggets they won't seem like lessons.

Paul's next book "Shoot and Aim Later" is planned for launch in the fall of 2017.

www.ingramcontent.com/pod-product-compliance
Lightning Source LLC
Chambersburg PA
CBHW021428170526
45164CB00001B/137